THE COMPLETE ILLUSTRATED GUIDE TO CASTING

THE COMPLETE ILLUSTRATED GUIDE TO CASTING

by

Joe Brooks

DOUBLEDAY & COMPANY, INC.
GARDEN CITY, NEW YORK
1963

To West Jordan,
the greatest rod maker of them all.

ACKNOWLEDGMENTS

Grateful acknowledgment is hereby given to Bill Browning, Montana State Chamber of Commerce, for the photos used in the chapter on fly fishing; to Francis "Johnny" Johnson, Florida State News Bureau, for the photos used in the section depicting heavy plug casting; to Jack and Dick Woolner, of the Massachusetts Game and Fish Department for the photos used in the surf-casting series; and to my wife, Mary, for those illustrating spinning and light plug casting.

My thanks also, to my friends Charles K. Fox, Edward "Luke" Gorham, Gordon Dean, Hal Lyman and Frank Woolner, who worked cheerfully for many hours in the production of the pictures, and contributed generously of their wide knowledge of the fields of angling in which each is especially expert.

I also wish to thank the editor and publisher of *Outdoor Life* magazine for permission to include herein information which has appeared in their pages from time to time.

CONTENTS

PREFACE

Good casting is the key to more fishing fun. Whatever the choice of weapon, whether wispy trout rod or the stout sticks used in heavy surf, the angler who knows how to handle his equipment, who learns to cast better than the average man, will definitely catch more fish and will also get a very real pleasure simply from casting, day in and day out, whether the fish are hitting or not.

From the moment you pick up the rod to the moment the lure hits the water, each step in the execution of the cast plays an important part. One missing link can throw the whole effort into confusion. As in golf, your stance, the way you hold your hands, rhythm and timing are all-important.

In many years of answering questions from readers and of teaching friends my favorite method of casting—the use of the fly rod—I have found that "*Show* me how!" is the request that crops up most often. With this in mind, I have selected a man I consider to be an expert practical fisherman in each of the casting methods and in the following pages he shows his way of handling his chosen equipment. With these pictures as a guide the novice can soon teach himself to cast and those who are already proficient may be able to pick up some pointers also, from the capable casters shown. In each case the photographs were made under actual fishing conditions, the better to illustrate the points being established. But your basic practice can be done at home on lawn or over swimming pool, in a gymnasium, or anywhere you can find room to make a cast. Then when you go where the fish are, you can fish with confidence, knowing that you are ready to make the utmost of your equipment and hence get the most out of it. I hope that this book will be a quick road to better casting and more fun in fishing, for everyone.

Joe Brooks

PART I
FLY CASTING

INTRODUCTION

From 50 feet away I watched the angler lift the rod tip slowly, bringing it back and upward in an effortless manner. The line came slowly off the surface and at 35 feet all the line had cleared and the leader was moving upward and then only the fly was on the water, traveling so slowly that it left no appreciable wake.

Now the angler's arm was at shoulder height, wrist out and slightly down, elbow slightly crooked. Then he gave a hard upward and backward flip of the wrist, raising his arm well up at the same time. He stopped the elbow at head height. Back of him the line rolled over high; line, leader, and fly moving in a wide loop.

Then he dropped his elbow a smooth 5 or 6 inches. His wrist came out of the two o'clock position and drove forward, putting force into the throw, so I could see the bend of the rod, well down into the middle section. He aimed his cast above the parallel to the water. As the line started forward he gave his wrist the last thrust, like hammering a nail at head height. Then he stopped the rod at the ten o'clock position.

Coil after coil of line shot out from the loosened fingers of his left hand, smoothly following the pull of the outgoing line through the guides. It turned over nicely in a perfect loop and straightened out as it reached the end of its journey, so that the leader went straight out and stopped with a bump as the shooting line came tight onto the reel spool.

Immediately coils started making up in the checked line and it fell quietly to the surface in the S-shaped, serpentine manner that promised a perfect, drag-free float for at least 4 feet. The dry fly floated jauntily along, wings gayly cocked, a beautiful thing for an angler to see and a challenge to any trout.

Such perfect execution of a cast calls for both skill and practice, but no more so than in any other sport. For all too many years fly casting has been regarded as the hard way to fish. Too many experts have stressed the fancy throws, the difficult ones, the trick casts, making it a mystic art, with the result that the average angler has come to regard fly casting as something beyond him with his average skill and average amount of time to put on the sport. If he sallies forth at all with the long, light rod, he ends up with the line around his

13

own neck or the fly caught in the seat of his fishing partner's pants. Naturally he soon decides that however wonderful, fly fishing is not for him.

Well, there's no doubt that fly fishing is the ultimate in angling, both as to style and execution. It does take skill and it takes concentration. But it brings to the caster many rewards not associated with other methods of fishing. The capable flycaster gets great satisfaction from his well-matched equipment, just as a golfer does from well-balanced clubs. He gets a big kick from a well-placed cast, whether or not it produces a fish. The simple act of turning in a good performance is its own reward. He thrills at the execution of a good cast that drops his fly on a dime under some overhanging tree limb or along the edge of some water cress where the sweeping current will carry it over the feeding station of some wise old brownie. His low cast into the wind, successfully performed, is every bit as satisfying as a low-hit tee shot. His curve to the left that makes the fly turn as if on a track, around some obstacle, to reach a spot where a wide-mawed buster of a fish is waiting, is akin to the pleasure of producing a similar curve to the left with a No. 2 iron. There are many things in fly fishing that remind the sportsman of golf and that is why so many golfers are good fly fishermen: they are used to a game that calls for a little practice to develop the skill that produces complete satisfaction with the game.

One of the saddest sights to be encountered is that of the man who has a two-week vacation, spends a good deal of money to get to the spot where he wants to fish, and then finds that he does not have the skill to cast well enough to take fish. Terrain or weather, or both, get the better of him. Yet a little practice in advance, over lawn or pool, would give him the proficiency to take fish under almost any circumstances.

The following pictures and descriptive text are offered in the hope that by looking at the pictures of each cast and reading how it is done, the prospective flycaster will absorb some of the idea behind the game before he even picks up a rod. Maybe they'll stir him to a few hours of practice so that when opening day dawns he'll be confident in his handling of his equipment, ready to "give the fish a fit."

Shown here are the casts most needed in all-round fly fishing, casts that sometime or other, if properly executed, will get the angler more and bigger fish. They apply to all kinds of fly fishing, on small streams and ponds, on lakes and big rivers, or in salty lagoons, bays, flats and even the Gulf Stream, because aside from the size of the tackle used, fly casting is the same under almost all circumstances. Most of the pictures were taken under actual fishing conditions, and all were made not with tackle stepped up for extra long or fancy

14

throws but with standard rods, reels, and lines, the kind of tackle the average fisherman will use.

Basic to all fly casting is a well-matched outfit. Trying to cast with a mismatched rod and line has been the cause of many a beginner giving up in disgust. If he had started with the right outfit he would soon have gotten the swing of it. Each angler will have to choose the rod most suited to his own needs, probably according to the kind of fishing in his own bailiwick. Once that choice has been made, the line should be selected to match.

In general, a 7½-foot rod, lined with an HEH (DT5F) line is suitable for small streams; an 8-foot rod with HDH (DT6F) line for larger trout waters; an 8½-foot rod with GBG (DT9F) or GBF (WF8F) line for big rivers and lakes when using large streamers and bucktails, and in many cases this same rod fits salmon fishing in smaller rivers. The 9½-foot rod matched with a GAF (WF9F) line is perfect for Atlantic salmon and sea trout and for handling poppers for largemouth bass in areas where there is lots of wind. This is also the best rod and line for all salt-water fly fishing.

CHAPTER 1 BASIC CASTS

HOW TO HOLD THE ROD

There are several ways to hold a fly rod, but to me only two of them give the necessary wrist freedom. The hand may go around the cork grip, with the fingers under and coming up on the inside and the thumb lying lightly along the top of the grip, as shown in picture No. 1; or the rod may be held in much the same manner but more as the right hand would hold a golf club, thumb and finger forming a V, so the thumb is further down on the side of the grip, as shown in picture No. 2.

This latter is the freer and less tiring of the two grips. It gets more power into the cast because the back of the hand is in such a position that it tells heavily in the pickup and the forward thrust of the rod. It makes for a free action of the wrist, which in turn delivers an effortless, smooth cast.

The grip should always be light. As in all sports, relaxation makes for better co-ordination and hence a smooth delivery. Instead of trying to squeeze the cork right off the rod, pick it up lightly, between thumb and first finger, as shown in picture No. 3, and let it settle gently into place, then close the hand lightly around it.

PICTURE NO. 1

PICTURE NO. 2

PICTURE NO. 3

17

WRIST POSITION

One of the most common faults with beginners is that of breaking the wrist backward so that not only the line but the rod tip itself will hit the water in back of them. If the caster should follow through with a forward cast then, from such a backcast, there would be nowhere for the line to go but up in the air. Many flycasters advocate stopping the rod "at one o'clock," that is, angled from the wrist in such a position that the rod would be pointing at 1 on the face of a clock, as shown in picture No. 4. I will go a step further and say stop at two o'clock. In casting on the stream, most fly fishermen, myself included, often go much further back than that and still get off a good throw. Tournament casters often go so far back that their rod parallels the ground. But to handle line from such a position calls for completely true timing, and until he is sure of this the caster should aim at the two o'clock position as his ideal. Then, when he makes his forward throw, the bend of the rod will work for him, giving the action needed to get the line off on its journey.

PICTURE NO. 4

HOW TO GET OUT LINE

The first thing the fly fisherman must do in order to present his fly to the fish is to get line out from his reel so that he can make a cast. To do this, he takes the fly in his left hand, holding it by the bend of the hook as shown in picture No. 5, so a sudden motion will not drive it into his fingers. Then he pulls the leader and about 6 feet of line out through the guides—enough so he can work it back and forth in the air.

Now, with line and leader in front of him, he makes a backcast,

PICTURE NO. 5

19

still holding the line tight in the fingers of his left hand, and with that hand pulling a couple more feet of line off the reel, as shown in picture No. 6, makes a false cast back, as shown in picture No. 7, and comes forward again, letting the line held in the left hand go. The line will shoot out, and again he pulls a couple of feet of line from the reel and sends that out on the next forward throw. All this time the line is in the air, hasn't touched the ground or water, and

PICTURE NO. 6

after four or five such movements he will have enough line out to make a cast.

After he has mastered getting out a few yards of line in this manner and wants further distance, he may strip more line from the reel and hold it in loops in his left hand. Then the line is retrieved to within 25 feet of the caster, picked up, false cast a couple of times and then shot out, and the released loops will go along with it.

PICTURE NO. 7

With 30 to 35 feet of line on the water in front of him, the angler is ready for the pickup. The rod is pushed out in front at arm's length but with the elbow slightly bent, then the rod tip is raised slowly, up and slightly back. Meantime, the line is held tight in the fingers of the left hand. When line and leader are both entirely out of the water and just the fly remains on the surface, as shown in picture No. 8, a hard, upward and backward flip of the wrist lifts the fly into the air.

All too many fishermen end their chances of taking fish when they snatch a great length of line from the water, with consequent noise and splash, as shown in picture No. 9. Trying to lift so much line only results in a poor backcast and poorer forward throw, besides scaring the spots off the trout and putting them down for a long time.

PICTURE NO. 8

One of the most important parts of the pickup is the position of the wrist. With line off the water and fly moving slowly along the top, the rod should be at shoulder height and wrist straight out toward the fly but held slightly over the grip and downward, while the elbow is relaxed, as shown in picture No. 10. This position of the wrist is just right for the backward and upward flip and allows the caster to stop the rod at the two o'clock position with ease; and it is also the perfect position for a strike if a fish should hit at the last split second before the pickup.

PICTURE NO. 9

PICTURE NO. 10

THE HIGH BACKCAST, ELBOW DROP, AND FORWARD THROW

After the pickup, the line is in back of the angler, high in the air, as shown in picture No. 11, turning over in a loop, and he is ready to start the forward cast by dropping his elbow about 6 inches and bringing the wrist forward as if to hammer a nail at head height, as shown in picture No. 12, the throw being aimed above the parallel to the water.

The cast should never be made with elbow held high as shown in picture No. 13. This is where it takes a combination of the forearm,

PICTURE NO. 11

PICTURE NO. 12

the back of the hand, and the bend of the rod to start the cast off well.

Once the forward impulse has been imparted to the line the rod should follow through to about the ten o'clock position. There it is stopped and held as the line drops to the surface, as shown in picture No. 14.

This forward throw is the basis of all casts. The many variations, the curves, rolls, and hauls, are merely trimmings that help to take fish in difficult situations, and they will not be mastered until the forward throw has become automatically sound.

PICTURE NO. 13

PICTURE NO. 14

CAST ABOVE THE PARALLEL

The main thing to remember in making the forward throw is not to cast at the surface of the water. Such a low aim prevents the achievement of any distance because the line falls, or rather plows, into the surface before its forward impulse is spent, and piles up on itself, as shown in picture No. 15. Rather, the angler should aim a foot or two above the parallel to the water, as shown in picture No. 16, and watch the line go out, roll over, and stop.

PICTURE NO. 16

DON'T "BREAK" THE WRIST

To achieve a good forward throw, the wrist must be in a strong position, at one or two o'clock, just prior to starting the forward cast. If the wrist is "broken" as shown in picture No. 17, the rod almost reaches the water behind the caster and the line drops onto the surface as shown in picture No. 18, adding weight and throwing the outfit off balance so that a good forward throw is impossible. If the caster is able to get off any throw at all it will only go up, as shown in picture No. 19, because the line is too far down behind him to be whipped by the rod into a sufficiently parallel position to make a true throw.

PICTURE NO. 17

PICTURE NO. 18

PICTURE NO. 19

29

HOW TO RETRIEVE

For all-round efficiency the strip method of retrieve is the best. With the rod grip in the right hand, thumb and middle or first finger extended toward the inside, the line is pulled through them with the left hand, as shown in picture No. 20. The strip may be an inch in length or a foot, and the line so gathered in may be looped in the left hand as shown in picture No. 21.

As the left hand is moved from the line to make the next strip, thumb and finger of the right hand are in position to clamp down and hold the line taut in case of a strike, until once again the left hand grasps the line.

This strip method of pulling in line allows for a very slow retrieve or a fast one, short jerks or long, according to need, and all the time

PICTURE NO. 20

the angler is ready for a strike or to pick up for the next cast. During the retrieve the rod is pointed in the direction of the fly but slanted up so that the tip can absorb the shock of a strike. If the tip were pointed right at the water, and a fish hit, the leader might readily break.

Many trout anglers use the figure 8 retrieve, bringing the line in by finger manipulation in such a manner that it forms a figure 8 in the palm of the left hand. This is done by grabbing the line with the fingers of the left hand and turning the hand each time a small length of line is pushed into the palm, then holding the palmed line with the thumb as fingers again reach out for more line. It is possible to shoot line very nicely when held in this manner, but the speed of the retrieve is greatly limited, and especially where action must be imparted to the fly it is not nearly as efficient as the strip method.

PICTURE NO. 21

WATCH THE BACKCAST

A lot of practice can be wasted if you don't know what's going on behind you. The quickest way to find out is to watch that backcast. In picture No. 22 angler turns to watch his backcast to see whether it's going up or down or straight out behind him. A few minutes spent keeping the line in the air with false casts, and turning each time to watch the line roll out behind you, will soon improve timing.

PICTURE NO. 22

THE HORIZONTAL CAST

Sometimes a fish is rising in a small pool in such a spot that it seems impossible to get a fly over him. There are low-hanging bushes coming within 4 feet of the surface of the water. More tree limbs crowd the angler from behind. It looks hopeless—but "'t ain't necessarily so!" For he can kneel down and strip out 20 feet or so of line from the reel, then pull the leader and several feet of fly line out through the guides. Then, holding the rod horizontally, as shown in picture No. 23, he can false cast and by forceful wrist action can obtain great speed to keep the line in the air, not too high, so it would catch on branches, not too low, so it would catch on the ground or touch the water. When he has enough line out to reach the rising fish, he can make the throw, shoot the line, again horizontally, and wait for the strike.

This cast does not allow the fly to be dropped lightly and many times, in spite of all your care, it will catch on the trees, but all in all, if used carefully, it will take many trout that would otherwise be missed. It is a good throw for getting under bridges or other over-hangs, as well as trees and bushes.

The main thing to remember is that the great line speed is needed to keep the line on an even keel as it goes back and forth so it will not hang up on anything, which, of course, is exactly what would happen if a regular cast were used.

PICTURE NO. 23

THE ROLL CAST

The roll cast is needed many times in the course of a day astream. It is an easy cast to perform and pays off heavily, especially if there are trees behind the angler to prevent a backcast. To execute the roll, the angler brings the line in until he has about 25 or 30 feet of line on the surface in front of him. The thing to remember here is to keep that

PICTURE NO. 24

PICTURE NO. 25

34

line in front of you on the water to supply purchase when the forward roll is begun.

When the rod has come back to the two o'clock position, as shown in picture No. 24, it is brought forward in very much the same way as when performing the regular forward cast, but with more follow-through from hand and rod, sharply down, stopping about 3 feet from the surface. The line will follow the rod, roll on out, as shown in picture No. 25, and flip the fly over to land beyond line and leader. The back view of the same cast, shown in picture No. 26, illustrates how the tip of the rod gets into the action at the very moment the angler starts the roll cast. Rod tip is snapping forward and picking up line from the surface, preparatory to rolling on out.

PICTURE NO. 26

BACKHANDED ROLL CAST

Though not often needed, this cast is a lifesaver when the angler finds himself crowded by brush as he fishes along the right bank of a stream. The technique of making the throw is the same as for the straightaway roll cast, the difference being in hand and rod position. The rod is taken with the regular grip, then arm and wrist are brought across the body to the left, so the rod is at about a 35-degree angle and with the back of the hand toward the body. This allows the angler to get a free wrist into the cast and gives him the full power of the back of his hand. The cast is then delivered as in the regular roll. There is no exact rod position just before the roll is made, as the caster must adjust slightly for wind (as shown in picture No. 27, where the rod is held slightly higher to compensate for wind blowing line out to the left) or for the line being carried downstream by currents.

PICTURE NO. 27

ROLL CAST FROM A HIGH BANK

Many times the angler finds himself on a high bank with trees close behind him. This is the moment for another variation of the roll cast. At such a height above the water, special attention must be given to the end of the cast. The line is brought in in the same way but with the rod held a little farther forward, then the rod is moved slowly up to the two o'clock position and then thrust forward, as in picture No. 28. The main difference comes right at this point. From here the rod must be brought right down to the surface in order to flatten out the roll which the line is forming and which, when the angler is at such a height, would drop the fly almost directly in front of him if the rod were not thrust down. But the down push drives the circle into an oval and allows the fly to go out much farther.

PICTURE NO. 28

ROLL-CAST PICKUP

The roll-cast pickup is the ideal way of getting line in the air again as it comes floating downstream in fast water, as for instance in picture No. 29. The line floats so fast sometimes that the angler cannot retrieve quickly enough, and the line moves in at such speed it may foul up on rod or even on the angler himself and he cannot get a tight line for the pickup. Picture No. 30 shows the angler in this unfortunate position, unable to get a tight line, bound to end up in a tangle.

The roll-cast pickup overcomes this difficulty by pushing the line out instead of pulling it in, as does the ordinary pickup. That is, the angler allows the line to float down the distance he wishes, or to the point beyond which he figures he won't get a strike from a fish. Picture No. 31 shows him in this position, rod held high, line coming in on the water—the right spot for the roll-cast pickup. Now he brings the rod up and back to the two o'clock position, as in the regular roll cast, and then down into the forward thrust as shown in picture No. 32. Then, before the line has time to drop to the surface, he brings the rod back again in a conventional backcast and out again in a forward throw for another try at the fish, as shown in picture No. 33.

PICTURE NO. 29

PICTURE NO. 30

PICTURE NO. 31

39

PICTURE NO. 33

40

THE AERIAL ROLL CAST

The aerial roll cast is used when the angler finds himself in a covelike spot with trees forming a bank behind him as well as on both sides, so that he has no room whatever for even the shortest of backcasts. It is also useful when the wind is blowing so hard that it knocks the backcast down or is so strong as to prohibit a backcast of enough line to get a good forward throw.

To execute the aerial roll, the angler starts the line off with the same wrist and rod action as if he were going to do the regular roll cast. Picture No. 34 shows the position for the pickup. Picture No. 35 shows the beginning of the roll. Now, with line in the air, instead of letting it fall to the surface, he keeps it rolling in the air by means of a circular motion of the wrist, as shown in picture No. 36, until he is ready to make the cast. Then, line still in air, he makes the forward cast, bringing the wrist forward, then following through and letting the line shoot outward to the spot where he intends it to hit. It does not make for a long-distance cast but it will get out 40 feet and that is often plenty to catch fish.

PICTURE NO. 34

PICTURE NO. 35

PICTURE NO. 36

HOW TO MAKE THE FLY DROP TO THE SURFACE BEFORE THE LINE

While no caster consistently achieves the ideal of the fly always lighting ahead of the leader and line, there are many times when it is most important that it should do so, for instance on a very quiet pool where you want to avoid a hard line slap that would scare the fish. The cast used to cause the fly to light first is very much like the curve to the left, the only difference being in the rod position at start and finish of the cast. The rod is held up and out a bit from the perpendicular, then the regular forward cast is made harder than needed for the distance to be covered. When the fly gets out above its destination, the angler pulls back with the rod tip to the position shown in picture No. 37.

The line will come to a stop and bounce off the reel, the force of the halt holding the line suspended out straight for a moment. Then leader and fly will snap down to the water, very much like a drop in baseball. And the line falls softly down a moment later.

PICTURE NO. 37

CHAPTER 2   PRACTICAL LINE AND ROD WORK

HOW TO SHOOT THE LINE

Shooting the line means throwing out more line on the forward cast than the angler picks up from the water, or has been false casting. It allows him to get the fly out faster to an oncoming fish than he could if he had to make several false casts in order to get out line for the required distance. It also allows the flycaster to fish all day without developing a tired arm. Constant false casting with a bass-bugging outfit, for instance, or with big, wind-resistant streamers or bucktails and a 9- or 9½-foot rod and a GAF (WF9F) line—constant false casting with such an outfit can be brutal, and more so if there is a strong wind blowing.

But shooting the line makes fly casting easy regardless of conditions or the outfit used. And with the ultralight dry fly outfit it is essential, because being able to shoot the line means that the angler can reach the fish without excessive motion to frighten them.

To execute the shoot, the line is held in coils in the left hand as shown in picture No. 38, where the backcast has just been begun. The backcast is made and the forward cast begun, and then, as soon as the forward thrust is made, the looped line is released from the left hand. The weight and momentum of the forward-moving line will pull the loops out and through the guides as shown in picture No. 39, and at the end of the cast, as shown in picture No. 40, there is nothing left of the loosely looped line.

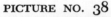

PICTURE NO. 38

When fishing from a skiff, the line may be dropped in the bottom of the boat rather than held in coils. In such case, a piece of carpet or linoleum in the bottom will preserve the line finish, or a landing net placed flat in the bottom will serve the same purpose. Some anglers also drop the loose line on the water when wading, or on the bank if walking, and count on the momentum of their cast to carry it out. However it is done, the line gets out there fast and with a minimum of effort.

PICTURE NO. 39

PICTURE NO. 40

HOW TO SHOOT THE BACKCAST

The backward shoot is used when the angler already has 30 to 35 feet of line on the water and wants to get more distance immediately, either to avoid false casting in order to save his arm, or to reach an oncoming fish before it gets close enough to see him and be frightened. This cast is so useful that, once it has been mastered, the angler will find himself using it automatically, nearly all the time.

Holding the extra looped line in the left hand, the angler picks up line from the water and as the backcast rolls out he releases some

PICTURE NO. 41

of the looped line from the left hand, as shown in picture No. 41. The combined weight of the 35 feet of line and the speed of the pickup will pull it on out for several more feet, as shown in picture No. 42. Then the angler clamps down with the fingers of his left hand again to stop the backward impulse, makes the forward throw, and shoots the rest of the loops on the cast itself, just as in shooting the forward cast under ordinary conditions. It is possible to control 10 to 15 feet of line on this backward shoot, and thus add a very considerable distance to the forward throw.

PICTURE NO. 42

HOW TO MEND THE LINE

Fish lie facing into the current and they like to see the fly coming downstream, free-floating and broadside. Many times they will be lying in such a position that to present the fly to them in the way they like, without drag, the line must be mended. To do this, the cast is made across stream, or a little up and across, according to the lie. It may float free for a moment, then the current will take hold of the heavy fly line and put a downstream belly in it, as shown in picture No. 43, thus putting drag on the fly and causing it to skid sideways or race downstream, moving faster than the current.

To avoid this heavy line pulling leader and fly after it, the rod is pushed out in the direction of the cast and parallel to the water. Then, with a twist of the wrist from right to left or left to right, as the case may be, in a slow flip, a half roll is imparted to the line, outward and slightly upward, as shown in picture No. 44. This causes the line to leave the water and roll several feet upstream before it falls to the surface again. And when it does, there it is, in reverse position as far as the current is concerned. The belly is now UPstream, as shown in picture No. 45, and this allows the fly 3 or more feet of good float before once again drag sets in and another mend is called for.

This cast takes some practice in order to avoid moving the fly when the mend is made, but it is a very important part of fly fishing, whether with dry fly, nymph, streamer or wet fly. And with a little practice plus a well-greased, high-floating line, it can soon be mastered

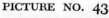

PICTURE NO. 43

PICTURE NO. 44

PICTURE NO. 45

49

HOW TO DO THE LOW CAST INTO THE WIND

The low cast into the wind, also called the wind cheater, is just about a must for flycasters and it is not difficult to do. With rod held off to the right at an angle of about 45 degrees, the usual backcast is made, the forward cast begun, and the looped line held in the left hand is released. Then the elbow is dropped as in the regular forward cast but the rod is continued on through, fast, and with an extra push as it nears the water. At the same time the wrist is turned over a bit, to the left, bringing the rod tip down to within a foot of the surface of the water, as shown in picture No. 46.

The line will go straight out, the end of line and leader staying flat instead of turning over in the usual wide loop, and the fly will be smartly flipped out in spite of the wind.

This cast is especially good with a very light outfit, when distance is needed, because even the slightest breeze can play havoc with a 9- to 14-foot leader. But the low, into-the-wind cast, plus the added push of the double haul to give more power and line speed, will get it out there right into a fairly stiff wind, and with an ease that is surprising.

PICTURE NO. 46

HOW TO DO THE GRASSHOPPER OR BUMP CAST

When bushes or tree limbs hang down to within a foot or two of the water, it is often difficult to get a fly under and in where the angler suspects a lunker is lying. But usually the bump or grasshopper cast will do the job. This cast is delivered in the same manner as a low cast into the wind, but with the rod held more to the right and almost parallel to the water. Then the cast is aimed at the bottommost limbs and thrown hard. The fly hits the water with great force just in front of or just under the tree limbs and the momentum of the cast makes the fly hop forward another foot or two, on into the pocket where the lunker is hiding. The important thing to remember with this cast is to be sure to shoot the line. If the line is held, it will roll upward at the end in a wide bow, and hang up on the bushes.

In picture No. 47, the bump cast has just been delivered and the line has fallen to the surface. The tracks on the water show that the fly hit well outside the overhanging limbs, skipped once like a thrown flat stone, then came to rest well back in. Note that the rod is a bit below the parallel to the water at the end of the cast. The next move on the angler's part will be to raise the rod tip slightly to cushion a hard strike.

PICTURE NO. 47

HOW TO DO THE DOWNWIND CAST

When a strong wind is blowing from behind, the angler often has difficulty in getting off a good throw because the backcast is buffeted down by the wind. The easiest way around this is to shorten the backcast to about 15 feet, allow it to fall behind, almost to the surface, and then make the forward cast upward. The line will move up, clearing the angler's head, and when it has gone on out, he stops the rod at the eleven o'clock position and shoots the line. The wind will then take it on out and at the end of the cast the line will come straight, parallel to the water, and then drop on down.

In picture No. 48, the line in back of the angler is moving upward as the forward thrust is made. It will carry on up over his head and on up beyond the rod tip to the line limit, then the wind will blow it forward its entire length. Then, as the rod is stopped in pictured position, the line will straighten out, stop, and fall to the water.

Another way of doing the downwind cast is to use a horizontal cast but throw the backcast well behind, toward the angler's left, then make the forward cast by aiming the wrist outward and casting well to the right instead of straight ahead. The line will curve out to the right but the force of the wind will push it around almost straight downwind.

PICTURE NO. 48

HOW TO AVOID CROSS-WIND TANGLES

Many an angler has known the frustration of trying to get off a cast when the wind is blowing hard across him from right to left, so that his backcast is always carried in behind him and when he makes the forward throw he catches his shirt, his shoulder, or his cap. Instead of fighting this wind drift, it is possible to take advantage of it by slowing down the start of the forward cast just a fraction. This allows the line to drift freely to the left as shown in picture No. 49. Then the angler aims at the spot he wants to reach, makes his usual forward throw, but with the rod slanted a little over his head to the left, as shown, and line and fly will come through right over his head or a bit to the left and go straight out to the spot desired. For better placement, the rod tip is brought down hard, as in the low cast into the wind.

PICTURE NO. 49

HOW TO CAST ACROSS INCOMING FAST WATER

At the head of a pool where fast water comes piling in, fish often lie in the slow water beyond the current. If the fly is dropped on the far side in the usual manner, the fast incoming current will belly the line downstream so fast that it will snatch the fly out of there before any trout has a chance to see it. Because of the heavy current, the line mend is not effective either.

To overcome this drag of the near, heavy water, the cast is made across to the other side and then the rod is held as high as possible, at full arm's length, as shown in picture No. 50. This lifts the line completely out of the water so that only the leader and fly float gently over the trout's lie. By this means 3 or 4 feet of free float can be obtained in this difficult position, and 3 or 4 feet is plenty to get hits from a trout. And in the position described, the angler is ready either to strike or to pick up for the next cast, with a simple wrist motion.

PICTURE NO. 50

HOW TO DO THE CHANGE-OF-DIRECTION CAST TO THE RIGHT

Here is another of the great pay-off casts. It will pull fish out of many tight places that would be out of reach of a straightaway throw. It is invaluable when a high bank or trees and bushes lie close behind and prevent a backcast. Suppose the angler is fishing upstream along the left bank and finds himself backed up against heavy foliage so there is no room for a backcast. He sees a fish rising 40 feet out in the stream, directly opposite him.

With back turned somewhat toward the shore, he makes his usual up- and down-stream false casts to get line out, as shown in picture No. 51. Then, as he makes the throw, he pivots from the hips, left to right, and rolls his wrist slowly to the right, aiming at the spot where he wants the fly to light. The rod will follow his wrist around and point like a finger at that spot and the line will follow the curve of the wrist as if it were on tracks, as shown in picture No. 52, and go on out and put the fly down right where the angler wants it, as in picture No. 53.

By turning the wrist the desired amount, it is possible to cast at as great an angle as 90 degrees from the direction the angler is facing, and even with a great change of angle a distance of 50 to 55 feet can be obtained.

PICTURE NO. 51

The change-of-direction cast is useful when speed is essential, even when there is room for a backcast; for instance, when a cruiser is spotted off to the side and the angler is in the middle of his backcast. Without losing a second, he can continue his throw, turning his wrist to the desired angle and drop the fly right in front of that cruiser.

PICTURE NO. 52

PICTURE NO. 53

HOW TO DO THE BACKHAND CHANGE-OF-DIRECTION CAST

The change-of-direction cast can be done to the right or the left, upstream or down, and even backhand. For the latter, the arm is brought across the body and the hand laid, palm outward, fingers outstretched, across the face, as if to ward off a blow, as shown in picture No. 54. Now, when the rod is placed in the fingers, as shown in picture No. 55, you are in position to execute the cast: the same position, incidentally, as for a straightaway backhand cast.

The false casts are made up and down the stream, as shown in picture No. 56, and the last false cast prior to the final throw is allowed to roll right out and drop almost to the water. Then the forward throw is started, the angler aiming at the spot where the fly is to light by pointing his wrist at that spot. At the same time he pivots from the hips. As shown in picture No. 57, line and leader and fly will follow the course of the rod as if in a groove.

The important thing to keep in mind is that this cast must be done very slowly, almost in slow motion.

PICTURE NO. 54

PICTURE NO. 55

PICTURE NO. 56   PICTURE NO. 5

CHAPTER 3   ADVANCED CASTS

HOW TO DO THE DOUBLE HAUL

The next series of casts consists of the advanced throws that make fly fishing more fun and add extra fish to the creel. They are the throws that get the fisherman out of difficult spots and fill his days with satisfaction even if fish are few and far between. It must be remembered that they all stem from the basic forward cast and that this should be thoroughly mastered before the more advanced ones are attempted.

The double haul was developed by tournament casters to achieve new distance records, but this is not just a show cast. It is the fisherman's friend, enabling him to shoot the fly out even in a strong wind, providing the power to throw a big, wind-resistant popping bug a long way, taking the work out of casting so the angler can enjoy his sport all day without becoming tired.

The double haul is applicable to all kinds of fly fishing. It is wonderful when using a big outfit for salt-water fishing, and for bug fishing in sweet water. It is exceptionally good when using the lightest of outfits, a 3¾-ounce fly rod and HEH (DT5F) line, and a 14-foot leader tapered down 5X tippet and with a fuzzy dry fly on the end of it; for in this latter case it takes the power supplied by the double haul to

PICTURE NO. 58

get the line out and work up enough line speed to turn over that long, fine leader and fluffy fly instead of letting the whole thing collapse in a bird's nest.

To do the double haul, the angler takes hold of the line just below the butt guide, with his left hand, and pulls down smartly just as he begins the pickup, as shown in picture No. 58. At the same time, the pickup is finished with a good, hard, backward and upward flip of the wrist. This pull, coupled with the snap of the rod will give great speed to the backcast.

As the line speeds back, the left hand is allowed to drift up, as shown in picture No. 59, still holding the line to head height. Then the forward cast is begun with the rod hand, and at the same moment the left hand rips down hard on the line, as shown in picture No. 60. Then, when the forward impulse has been imparted to the line, the left hand releases it and all that line which has been stripped from the reel will shoot on out.

The important thing in this cast is the timing of the raising and pulling down of the left hand, which holds the line. The caster should

PICTURE NO. 59

practice each part of the cast separately, first the single haul as the line is picked up and thrown back, doing this over and over till he is satisfied he has the timing right on it. Then he can start drifting the left hand up with the line to shoulder or head height, ready to make the haul for the forward throw, and from there it is just a step to the completed haul. This getting of the left hand up to the pull-down position seems to be the most difficult part of the double haul technique, but if you take it easy, concentrate on what that left hand is meant to do, and keep practicing, you'll find the results are worth the time and effort.

PICTURE NO. 60

HOW TO CAST ACROSS AN OBSTACLE

When a log or some other obstacle juts out from the shore and a nice-looking fish is rising in the pool beyond, there's a good chance of downing him if you try to jockey into a safer casting position. With a little ingenuity you can take him right from where you are, simply by throwing a regular forward cast, dropping the fly about 3 feet above the fish and allowing the line to fall and lie lightly over the obstacle, as shown in picture No. 61. When the fish hits, the angler's strike will cause the line to jump up from the log, as you see happening in picture No. 62, and come tight between rod and fish, as in picture No. 63, and then the fight can be conducted as usual and the angler can steer the fish around the obstacle and land him.

If the fish does not take, the line and fly can readily be lifted out of there by means of the horizontal pickup, described later in this series, or it can be pulled in slowly and carefully and eased over the log without hooking it. Many times, if line and leader are moved in slowly this way, until only about 2 feet of leader remain on the other side of the log, then a quick, sharp yank will pull that bit of leader against the log, toss the fly into the air, and drop it on the near side of the log.

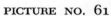

PICTURE NO. 61

62

HOW TO DO THE S-CAST

This cast, called the S-cast or serpentine cast, is used mostly when dry fly fishing in order to obtain slack line so that the fly may have several feet of free float before Ol' Devil Drag sets in. It may be used on upstream casts, up and across throws, or on straight downstream casts—anywhere, in fact, that a little extra free float is desired.

There are two good ways to make the S-cast. One is to get a good forward throw started, shoot the line, and, as it goes out, impart a side-to-side wiggle to the rod tip. This will send the line out in corresponding wiggles and it will drop to the surface in the S or serpentine formation.

The more generally used method is to make a straightaway throw with more steam than required to reach the spot where the fly is to drop. When the line is out over the desired place, the angler stops the rod high and pulls back on it smartly. This causes the moving line to bounce off the reel core and the jerk pulls it back so it drops to the water in a serpentine manner. As the fly drifts down the current, these coils will gradually straighten out, but until they do the fly has a nice free float over the trout the angler is after.

Picture No. 64 shows the end of such a cast. Note that the rod is held high after being stopped and pulled back an inch or two as the line was shooting out. Coils on the surface show how much free float will be possible before drag sets in. Also notice the curve in the line between rod tip and water—an S is forming there and when the rod tip is lowered the line will take on the shape of an S on the water.

PICTURE NO. 64

THE BOW AND ARROW CAST

This is not just a trick cast but one that the angler may find useful perhaps a dozen times during the course of a season, especially when fishing confined waters such as small pools along mountain streams where dense foliage hems him in, as shown in picture No. 65. And if such a cast will take a fish for him even half those times, it is certainly worth being able to do.

To make the cast, the fly is held in the left hand by the bend of the hook, while several feet of line are pulled off the reel. Then the

PICTURE NO. 65

hook hand is pushed well back of the angler, while the rod is brought forward so the line comes tight between rod and fly. Then a little more push on the rod forms the bow which gives the cast its name, as shown in picture No. 66.

To deliver the cast, the angler gives the rod a sharp forward flip, at the same time releasing the fly, and it goes out like an arrow from a bow, for the length of line stripped from the reel, plus the length of the leader. Because you are casting the light end of the fly line and the extra-light and long leader usually required in water where this cast would be used, it is important to give a good hard snap to the right wrist to get line speed, and make a smooth follow-through that will carry the rod tip down to within a foot of the water.

Usually this cast will only get out about 12 to 15 feet, but on small streams that is often enough to take trout.

PICTURE NO. 66

HOW TO DO THE HORIZONTAL PICKUP

Like the roll-cast pickup, this is one of the most valuable bits of maneuvering in the fly fisherman's repertory. There are many places where, unless he gets a strike on the first cast, he has no second chance because he can't get his fly back without disturbing the fish. For instance, when a fish is rising just beyond a patch of floating grass or matted weeds, the cast can be made so that the line falls on the weeds while the leader and fly, lighting just beyond, will get enough float to go over a trout. But if he doesn't take the first time, there the fly is, close against the grass and bound to hook up on it when the pick-up is made, as shown in picture No. 67.

This is the moment for the horizontal pickup, which will lift the fly straight up off the water in a corkscrew manner, and then a backward pull starts the line into the backcast, ready for another throw to that reluctant fish. And on the water there is no disturbance to make him think that that fly was anything but a natural that suddenly took wing.

To perform the horizontal pickup, the rod hand is turned so the back is down, parallel to the water, while the left hand holds the line tight so there can be no line slip. Picture No. 68 shows the close-up view of the hand position, while picture No. 69 shows the rod being lowered toward the horizontal, line beginning to tighten across the grass. From this position, the angler will give a quick forward and upward snap of the wrist and the rod tip will be continued on up to about a 45-degree angle. The line will roll forward over the grass and when the impulse reaches the fly, line, leader and fly will all go upward in a corkscrew motion, up 4 to 5 feet, as shown in picture No. 70, ready for the back pull and so into another cast.

PICTURE NO. 67

67

PICTURE NO. 68

PICTURE NO. 69

PICTURE NO. 70

68

THE STEEPLE CAST

The steeple cast is used mainly when no other cast will get the fisherman out of a box where there are trees plumb in back of him within a couple of feet. It sends the fly line straight up into the air for a considerable distance on the backcast, and the teaser is how to get it down again anywhere but on top of the angler's hat.

To do the steeple cast, the rod is grasped so that the back of the hand comes over the top of the grip and the palm of the hand is face down to the water. If the hold is correct, the angler will not be able to see the cork grip at all, just the back of his hand, as in picture No. 71. From this position, a quick upward flip of the wrist, along with a strong upward thrust of the entire arm sends rod and arm straight up, as in picture No. 72. Looks like a fisherman's version of the Indian rope trick! (Monkey has already climbed the line and disappeared.) At the tip of the rod it can be seen that the line is a little back of the vertical, which allows for a short forward cast.

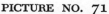

PICTURE NO. 71

69

Now the arm is slowly dropped and the forward cast is made with an exaggerated follow-through. This will usually produce a cast of 30 to 40 feet, which many times is enough to take fish. It's not a "good" cast, generally speaking, but it may come in handy once or twice a season, and it is one of those throws that flycasters like to be able to do just for the satisfaction involved.

THE CURVE TO THE RIGHT

The curve to the right (the angler's right) is especially popular with dry fly men, to send the fly down-current in front of fly and leader. One method of making the curve, especially when only a short-distance throw is required, say up to 40 feet, is to make the cast up-stream and finish without putting the tip into the cast. In other words, cast with the middle of the rod. The result is a sloppy curve to the right, as shown in picture No. 73, the line going out and falling with line and leader well to the right of the rest of the line because the final impulse of the rod tip is lacking. This cast will put the fly over the fish ahead of line and leader and with enough slack for a good 4- or 5-foot float.

A second way to throw a curve to the right is to use the change-of-direction cast, making the false cast up- and down-stream, then as the forward throw is started, turn the wrist to the point where the fly should land. As the end of the line and leader starts to roll over, shoot a couple of feet of line, and drop the rod tip a bit. The end of line and leader will curve to the right and drop lightly to the surface. Usually such a cast will send the fly down the current ahead of the line and leader.

PICTURE NO. 73

THE CURVE TO THE LEFT

The curve to the left is used quite often to avoid some obstacle. The rod is held out to the side at about a 40-degree angle, aimed slightly to the right of where the fly is to land. The cast is made with more force than required for the distance to be thrown, and when the line goes whistling out, then the rod is halted abruptly and even pulled back a little. This sudden stoppage causes the line to whip around to the left, dropping the fly on the spot desired. In picture No. 74 the line has fallen to the surface in the curve to the left and the angler is beginning to raise the rod tip, ready for a strike.

This cast will not set the fly down on a dime but it will put it within a foot or two of the spot the angler is aiming at. The aim must be fairly accurate, usually, in order to have the line fall clear of clutching tree branches or rocks, yet still have the end of the line and leader flip around the corner to the left.

PICTURE NO. 74

HOW TO DO THE REVERSE, OR GALWAY, CAST

The reverse, or Galway, cast is used when tall trees crowd the angler from behind and he needs a longer forward cast than he could get with either a steeple or a roll cast. Almost invariably, if he will scan the trees behind him he will find some spot where there is a hole in the foliage, a spot where he could let his line roll out if he could only be sure of not hooking the surrounding branches. So he turns his back to the stream, as in picture No. 75, and makes his forward cast, which can be made with greater accuracy than can a backcast—makes it up into the hole in the branches. When line and leader are rolling over, he pivots from the hips to face the river again, and at this moment the throw he has just completed becomes a backcast. He makes another forward cast and drops the fly on the water, as shown in picture No. 76. Timing and smooth pivoting are important, but can be acquired with a little practice.

A variation of this cast can also be done, without turning the entire body, by making the upward throw to the hole in the branches with a backhand cast, as shown in picture No. 77, watching the course of the line, and then, when it rolls over, simply turning the wrist and making the regular forward cast. But most anglers are not as accurate with their backhand cast as with the forward throw and are therefore more likely to hook up on one of the branches surrounding the safety area of that small hole among the trees.

PICTURE NO. 75

PICTURE NO. 77

HOW TO DO THE SHORT, SHORT CAST

With a very light outfit, say a 7½- or 8-foot rod, and HEH (DT5F) or HDH (DT6F) line and a 12- to 14-foot leader, there is so little weight to cast that it calls for special effort to get the fly out on a short-distance cast. And frequently the only way to reach a fish in certain quarters is to creep up on him and make a short cast. The same thing applies in many canals, irrigation ditches, and "jump across" streams, or when you need a quick toss to a fish that suddenly appears very close to you.

The short, short throw is done by making an extra-hard forward cast and following through by bringing the wrist down very hard, too, as if to drive the fly into the water. This will throw the light end of the line, the long, light leader and the often wind-resistant fly out far enough to get strikes. Picture No. 78 shows the finish of such a cast, with hard-driven line coming down almost to the water, and leader turning over to drop the fly.

PICTURE NO. 78

75

PART II
PLUG CASTING

CHAPTER 4   LIGHT PLUG CASTING

INTRODUCTION

In 1803 a watchmaker named George Snyder reluctantly moved from Bucks County, Pennsylvania, to Paris, Kentucky. He was an ardent trout fisherman and he hated to leave the clear streams of the Pennsylvania mountains, but business was business and so his fishing must needs suffer. But he soon found that Kentucky was better than he had anticipated for its lakes and ponds were filled with large and small-mouth black bass, fine game fish that were entirely new to him, as at that early date they had not yet been planted in Pennsylvania waters.

Snyder started out fishing for bass in the orthodox manner of the locals, using a long cane pole with minnows or frogs for bait. He caught plenty. But he kept seeing nice fish rising beyond the limits of an 18-foot cane pole and even out of reach of his fly rod. He soon set his precision-conscious watchmaker's mind to work on the problem and in 1805 he came up with the first quadruple multiplying reel ever made.

He put his amazing new invention on a short, stout rod and started fishing. The results were spectacular. As word got around, fellow anglers besieged him for reels like his own, offering almost any price for them. George obligingly made a few and gave them to his friends and before long other local metalworkers, seeing the possibilities of such reels, began to manufacture them commercially. Fishermen called them "bait-casting reels" because that was just what they did with them—cast bait, dead or alive.

As time went along, the reels were gradually improved and refined, but not for nearly a hundred years was their use extended beyond that original casting of bait. Then someone whittled a bit of wood into the shape of a minnow, fastened hooks on it, and artificial bait casting was born. "Plugs" they called these new-fangled fish foolers, and so evolved the term "plug casting," now more commonly used than the original term "bait casting."

The hand-carved plugs were soon followed by spoons, then by fly and spinner combinations with a bit of lead up front to give the weight needed for casting. Plug casting was on its way and now the fisherman could show his quarry a wide variety of items ranging through surface and underwater plugs, spoons, weighted bucktails, spinners with pork rind attachments, as well as an assortment of natural baits such as frogs, crawfish, minnows, hellgrammites, and night crawlers.

Such far-reaching equipment naturally increased the fishing pressure and soon the fish became more wary. In many lakes it became difficult to take them with a large plug that landed with a chunk, or a gob of bait plus lead that made a loud splash. Bass fishing began to be so short on reward that many anglers stopped going for them. Rumor said that the rivers and lakes were fished out. Only a few sharp-sighted anglers such as Ozark Ripley and Sheridan Jones suspected that the bass were as plentiful as ever, and as big, and that it was the angler who was at fault. They began the trend to longer, lighter rods and smaller baits for quieter delivery, figuring that these small plugs would hit the water with a lifelike spat and entice fish into hitting.

To Charlie Fox of Carlisle, Pennsylvania, goes the credit for pushing this trend to its logical conclusion, a long, light rod, fast reel, and lighter lines and bait. Not only is he a student of the use of this kind of tackle, (*Advanced Bait Casting* by Charles K. Fox, 1957, Putnam) but he is also one of the outstanding practical plugcasters in the country.

The lighter and faster the reel, the hotter it is to handle. A light-weight narrow spool with arbor is set into action easily and reaches a critical speed quickly. Therefore it requires exacting thumbing to prevent backlashes. A wider, heavier spool without an arbor starts into action more slowly and so does not as readily arrive at that critical speed which may produce a violent backlash early in the cast. It is therefore possible to push the heavier reels harder than the light ones, with less chance of trouble. For distances of over 100 feet the heavier reel would probably be the best, while for fishing from 40 to 100 feet, for instance working a shore line from a boat, or wading, the light, fast reel may prove more pleasant and do a better job. But for long-distance work, even with a ¼-ounce plug, the heavier reel with more power added will prove more effective. A cork or balsa-wood arbor will help this heavier reel send the light plug for long distances.

The new American-type fixed spool reels with push-button control allow the plugcaster to use even lighter lures. The drag on these enclosed-type reels can be set before casting and manipulated during the fight, and takes over the job the thumb performs with the regular plug-casting reel, to hold the line on the spool preparatory to making the cast, as well as supplying tension while fighting a fish.

Snyder's "short, stout rod" has carried through the years and plug-casting rods are still the shortest of the casting sticks. Six and a half feet is the maximum length that will travel through the casting arc fast enough to produce a long, flat cast; and ideally the length of the rod should be chosen to fit the weight of the lure to be used, but all should have plenty of backbone.

Standard rods for the various commonly used lure weights are:

  6¼-foot rod for ¼-ounce lure

  6-foot rod for ⅓-ounce lure

5½-foot rod for ½-ounce lure

5-foot rod for ⅝-ounce lure

However, the rod can be adapted for an off-weight lure. If the plug is too light, it can be dropped 6 to 12 inches from the rod tip and from that position the cast is made with extra effort. If the lure is too heavy, it is reeled in tight to the rod tip and the cast is made very lightly.

Lines must also be chosen to fit the lure: 7½-pound to 10-pound test for the ¼-ounce lures, 10- to 14-pound test for ½-ounce, and 14- to 18-pound test for ⅝-ounce. The minimum strength of line is based on the force used to throw the plug. In experiments with the straight-away throw, Charlie Fox found that the pressure exerted at the start of the forward cast is about 7 pounds—enough to break any line testing 6 pounds, but not that which tests 7½ pounds. Soft-finish braided lines are easier to handle than the treated hard braids, but the latter are more long lasting. Monofilament is excellent on the enclosed-type reels; and on the multiplying reel, limp monofilament is popular.

If braided silk is employed, a monofilament casting trace is used as the equivalent of the leader tippet in fly fishing. A 10-foot trace can easily be joined to the line with a barrel knot that will pass smoothly through the level wind. The greatest value of the slick trace is that it reduces friction on the tip guide at the start of the cast, thus allowing for greater distance, and it does not wear out near the lure. To cap it all, it is much less evident to the fish once the lure is in the water.

In the following pictures, Charlie Fox uses a 6¼-foot rod and a ¼-ounce lure to demonstrate the basic principles of plug casting.

THE BASIC FORWARD CAST

The Grip For the basic forward cast, the plug casting rod is held in a firm grip but with the muscles relaxed. Notice that there is no look of tension in Charlie Fox's arm, wrist, or hand, as shown in picture No. 1. The reel handles are up to give a minimum of friction and for free and smooth wrist action. The thumb rests against the line on the lower side of the reel.

This thumbing of the line is an important part of the plug-casting procedure, as the thumb pressure prevents the line from slipping out and allowing the lure to drop. The thumb holds the line throughout the entire mechanics of the backcast and up until the second on the forward cast when the angler releases it and lets the weight of the lure pull the line out after it.

PICTURE NO. 1

Sighting the Target   Charlie sights the target by lining it up with the lowest guide on the rod, as shown in picture No. 2. Arm is extended a bit, elbow down, thumb resting lightly on the spool, wrist cocked and ready to start the cast.

Picture No. 3 shows the caster as seen from the front, as he lines up the lowest guide on his rod with the target.

The Backward Thrust   Now, with an easy but forceful movement, he brings the rod back fast, the forearm moving backward and upward, stopping the wrist as the rod is at approximately two o'clock, as shown in picture No. 4.

PICTURE NO. 2

The Forward Delivery   In picture No. 5, he begins the forward motion of the rod, this forward motion being both faster and more forceful than the backward thrust. Terrific speed gets all of the rod into the cast. The thumb is still firmly pressed on the line to avoid any slippage and loss of power; and the wrist is set in position to deliver the forward thrust with force and smoothness.

Finish of Cast   As the rod comes through the ten o'clock position, the thumb is lifted off the spool, allowing the lure to move freely forward from the tip of the rod. In picture No. 6 the lure is on its way and the arm has been shoved out after it, wrist over, elbow high so the line will shoot out through the rod guides with the least possible friction. The thumb is moving upward to clamp down tight on the spool again at the upper edge, to stop the lure several feet above the surface, over the spot where it is intended to land. In picture No. 7, the lure has dropped to the surface. Note that the rod is held straight out, arm still extended, wrist on top of rod, and reel handles are up. If you will put yourself in the position of the caster, you will see that the lure has dropped precisely on the target sighted through the lowest rod guide.

PICTURE NO. 7

THE RETRIEVE

As the lure hits the water, the butt of the rod is brought in against the stomach as shown in picture No. 8 and the hold is quickly shifted to the left hand, which has moved forward on the rod so rod and reel rest in the heel of the hand. The left thumb takes over the job of maintaining pressure on the line in front of the reel to keep it tight until the right hand can grip the reel handles. Now, picture No. 9 shows Charlie Fox ready for the retrieve. Thumb and first finger of the left hand lightly control the line to tighten it for better spooling as it goes through the level wind and also to free the line from dirt or water that it may have picked up.

With the butt of the rod pressed against the stomach, the angler raises the rod to a 45-degree angle, so that it can absorb some of the shock if a fish should strike during the retrieve. From this position, as shown in picture No. 10, it is easy to convey action to the plug by means of short upward jerks of the rod. Some plugcasters hold the rod parallel to the water and out to either right or left, working the lure by imparting short; backward jerks. Others lower the tip almost to the surface and give small sideways jerks to the tip to make the lure spring forward in short skips on the surface or quick darts beneath the water. There are many ways to work a lure and the individual will find by trial and error which method suits him best, but the position shown in picture No. 10 is a sure and steady one from which to strike.

PICTURE NO. 8

THE STRIKE

When a fish hits, the rod is brought up smartly and with power, to ensure that the hook sinks in deep. As the strike is made, the handles of the reel are held tightly in the right hand, as shown in picture No. 11.

PICTURE NO. 11

88

SPECIAL CASTS TO MEET SPECIAL CONDITIONS

The most accurate cast is the straightaway throw, made with the rod moving in one groove, up and back and then forward in the same slot. But fishing conditions do not always permit this ideal cast and plugcasters have developed a number of throws to circumvent wind, bushes, or other obstacles or circumstances which might prevent an overhead cast.

Casting into the Wind   In the wind, even with a fairly heavy plug, it requires a little extra push if the angler is going to get the plug out where he wants it. To achieve that extra force, Charlie Fox brings the rod back to about a 45-degree angle, as shown in picture No. 12, instead of in the straight up and down path of the regular forward cast.

PICTURE NO. 12

Now he brings the rod forward in the same groove, hard, and at the same time turns his wrist so that the reel handles and the back of his hand are up. He drives down hard, releasing the spool at that exact second when the rod is parallel to the water, then continues the rod on down till the tip almost touches the water. At the same moment he comes down on his right knee, thus adding the drive of his whole body to that of the arm and wrist, to push the lure well out into the wind. This final position is shown in picture No. 13.

PICTURE NO. 13

The Sidearm Cast   There are many times when an angler must make his cast from the side rather than overhead, as for instance when trees lining a bank prevent a backthrust, or when he wants to cast low under tree limbs. Picture No. 14 shows angler ready to start a sidearm cast, rod held out in front in much the same position as for a regular cast, but down close to the parallel to the water.

In picture No. 15 he brings the rod back and to the side, arm extended so the rod stays just above the parallel to the water, the

PICTURE NO. 14

PICTURE NO. 15

thumb holding the spool to keep the lure at the desired distance below the rod tip. Picture No. 16 shows the wide angle at the peak of the backward thrust, just as the caster is about to begin the forward movement.

As with most casts, this forward movement is made with considerably more power than the backstroke. To put still more power into the cast, the wrist is turned over slowly and strongly. The beginning of this wrist movement is apparent in picture No. 17, and as

PICTURE NO. 16

PICTURE NO. 17

the arm sweeps on forward and up, as shown in picture No. 18, the wrist comes right over on top of the grip, the thumb releases the line and the lure is sent on out.

The right arm continues forward until the rod points at the target, as shown in picture No. 19, and the left hand moves up to take the rod so the right hand will be free for the retrieve.

This is also a very powerful cast to achieve long distance or for getting out into the wind.

PICTURE NO. 18

PICTURE NO. 19

The Backhand Cast   The backhand cast is convenient when trees or bushes on the right as well as above the angler prevent either a straightaway or a sidearm cast. It also comes in handy when you spot a rising fish and want to make a quick toss to him, or when you are crowded against a high bank and need to cast upstream. To execute this cast, Charlie reels the lure in tight against the end of the rod and extends his arm with elbow slightly bent, as shown in picture No. 20.

Now he brings the rod back across the body, just below the left shoulder, the elbow being bent so that the wrist and reel handles are automatically turned in toward the chest, as shown in picture No. 21. At this position there is a momentary hesitation, and then the forward swing is begun, the arm still maintained at a high level, and the rod being brought around with a hard snap of the wrist that pushes it to the right, as shown in picture No. 22. The caster will lift his thumb from the spool at the second he wishes to release the lure, and the thumb then moves up to the top of the reel to stop the line when the lure approaches the target.

At the end of the cast, as shown in picture No. 23, the arm is extended to the right, thumb is on the line at the top of the spool and the angler is ready to bring the rod butt down against his stomach, once again ready for the retrieve or to strike.

PICTURE NO. 20

PICTURE NO. 21

PICTURE NO. 22

The Silent Dive Cast   The silent dive cast is used to achieve a natural entry into the water with a minimum of noise, so that the fish will not be scared. While it is called "silent," actually the plug does make a sound as it hits the water but it is a "spat" rather than a splash,

PICTURE NO. 24

96

and sounds remarkably like the noise made by small baitfish as they feed. The sound is therefore more likely to attract larger fish than repel them.

This very productive cast is begun just like the regular forward cast illustrated in preceding pictures, but the angler uses an extremely flat trajectory to send the lure out without any excess of line between it and the rod tip. As the lure nears the end of its straight-out flight, the rod tip is raised slightly, as shown in picture No. 24, while the left hand comes up to the reel to grasp rod and line preparatory to retrieve.

At the same time that the line is taken between thumb and forefinger of the left hand, the thumb of the right hand clamps down on the reel spool and, as shown in picture No. 25, the rod is pulled back. The sudden stoppage of the lure causes it to come back toward the caster on a falling trajectory so it enters the water coming toward him, with the lifelike spat mentioned above. Picture No. 26 shows how the angler's whole body enters into this backward pull.

PICTURE NO. 25

97

He starts the retrieve at the height of the backward pull, as shown in picture No. 27, at the very moment the lure hits the water, thus finishing the natural dive with an enticing swimming action of the plug.

Once again he is in position to bring the rod butt down against his stomach for easy manipulation of the lure and a comfortable, forceful position from which to strike, as shown in picture No. 28.

PICTURE NO. 26

PICTURE NO. 27

The Underhand Lob   This cast is a sort of "toss," to get the plug into not-too-distant spots with a minimum of disturbance—places where an overhead throw or even the silent dive cast would drop too hard and because of the confined area might scare fish. The underhand lob puts the lure into the water on a slant, like a duck landing, skidding it forward on the surface with very little water disturbance.

The lob starts from the regular casting position, then, as shown in picture No. 29, the rod is started back to the side, rather than up. Picture No. 30 shows the peak of the backthrust, made slowly and smoothly, slanting down. Now, with the same slow, smooth motion, still keeping his thumb on the line spool, caster Fox starts the rod forward, but with rod and lure moving upward, as shown in picture No. 31.

PICTURE NO. 29

PICTURE NO. 30

The slow, smooth movement is continued on up and out and the thumb releases the line at about the position shown in picture No. 32. Note that, in contrast to most of the other casts described, in this one the wrist and handles of the reel are down and over to the right, so that the plug goes out under the level of the rod, thus achieving the skidding, skipping landing on the water. The wrist never turns over to the left.

The Flip Cast   Every angler has found himself in a spot where it seems there is no room whatever for a cast, either overhead or sidearm. In such a tight position, the flip cast is invaluable. It is also extremely useful when fishing canals and rivers, to shoot the plug into holes under a bank or in under low-hanging tree branches.

The first step in making the flip cast is to reel the lure tight against the rod tip. The slightest free swing away from the tip will make it almost impossible to do the flip cast. Then, as shown in picture No. 33, the rod is extended out in front of the caster at chest height.

102

103

Now a hard, downward motion is imparted to the rod, to bring the plug straight in at the angler's feet. This downward stroke naturally raises the elbow high, till it reaches the position shown in picture No. 34. When the rod has reached a position vertical to the angler's body, a forward flip, upward and outward, shoots the lure out

on a low, flat trajectory. Note that in picture No. 35 the forward flip has begun, the rod tip is leading the plug, which caster Fox will release at the point where his wrist begins to snap through, thus sending the lure out at the same level at which it now rides. Then the rod is continued on up until it reaches a position parallel to the water, as shown in picture No. 36, and once again the caster is ready to bring the rod butt down, for the retrieve position.

PICTURE NO. 36

AMERICAN ENCLOSED-TYPE PLUG-CASTING REEL

The only difference in performing the casts just described, while using an American enclosed-type plug-casting reel, is that the angler holds the line by touching a push button, as shown in picture No. 37, rather than thumbing the line. He releases the thumb, thereby automatically putting the reel in free spool at the instant he starts the forward cast.

PICTURE NO. 37

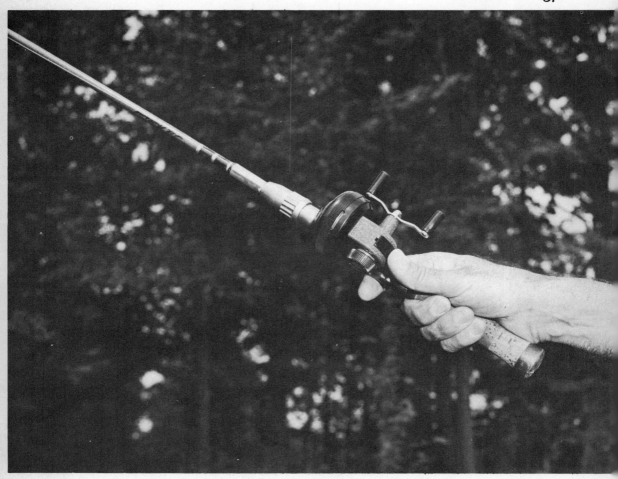

Charlie Fox's collection of plug-casting reels, old and new
Top, reading across—South Bend free spool, Gulf New Yorker, Bronson
Mercury
Second row, reading across—Gillian Neo Caster, Ambassador, Centen-
nial, Meek Blue Grass
Third row, reading across—Shakespear Sport Cast, Pflueger Akron,
Shakespear Beeyzel

CHAPTER 5   HEAVY PLUG CASTING

INTRODUCTION

For many years the use of heavy plug-casting gear was limited to a handful of fresh-water casters who went for muskies. But as much as twenty-five years ago, in the salty and brackish waters around Miami, a few anglers were also consistently using such outfits to do battle with big snook, redfish, barracuda, and tarpon. Away back then, a burnt thumb was the badge of the big-time plugcaster because with the older plug reels about the only way to slow a fish or hold one, or start him back, or to prevent overspin, was to thumb the line on the reel spool.

Eventually, thumb guards eliminated some of the throb in thumbs that had been pressed too long and too firmly on a whirling spool as some fish took off. Then manufacturers added a leather guard mounted on the reel, and still later they came up with a star drag on trolling reels and some of these reels, in the smaller sizes, were utilized for plug casting. However, because most fishing tournaments outlaw the use of the star drag, this never became popular with the majority of sport fishermen. Finally a reel was devised with a cub drag attachment, which is activated when the angler holds the reel handle and allows the fish to take line from the revolving spool while the handles are held stationary. When the handles are released, the reel operates in the conventional manner, so to avoid overspin the angler must keep alive to the lunges of the fighting fish by again holding one or both handles. In other words, there is direct contact between fish and angler during the fight and thus this is a more "sporting" reel, while at the same time eliminating the problem of the burnt thumb.

For the past fifteen years Jerry Coughlan of Boca Raton, Florida, has been catching tarpon up to and over 100 pounds while using this plug-casting gear, with 15- and 18-pound test line. He has taken perhaps 50 tarpon over 100 pounds and his best fish, a tremendous 161-pound 8-ounce silver king, is still the talk of the fishing fraternity, a terrific angling feat by this former crack miler of the Irish Olympic track team.

Some of the catches made by members of the famous Rod and Reel Club of Miami Beach during the past five years also belong in the phenomenal class. Using such an outfit and 15-pound test line, Luis de Hoyos of Monticello, New York, landed an 82-pound Pacific sailfish at Pinas Bay on Panama's west coast. Also at Pinas Bay, Moses Nunnally of Richmond, Virginia, caught a broomtail grouper that went 42 pounds, a new Rod and Reel Club record. Luke Gorham of Miami came up with a 38½-pound kingfish. Frank Violette of

Balboa, Canal Zone, took a 47-pound dogtooth snapper, only to be topped by Lou Koehler of Miami, with a hefty 57-pounder. Gar Wood Jr. added a terrific 103-pound shark to the list. And fishing at Islamorada on the Florida Keys, with Captain Jimmie Albright, Bart Foth of Gettysburg, Pennsylvania, brought in a jewfish that weighed 170 pounds, perhaps the largest fish ever taken on a plug-casting outfit.

So this type of casting has become increasingly popular with those who fish the salt for "whoppers," and has taken its rightful place in the fishing scene. It fills a need between the heavy spinning outfit and the light plug.

The rods used in heavy plug casting are made of either glass or bamboo and are commonly 6 feet 2 inches in length and weigh from 4 to 5½ ounces. These stout sticks are necessary to throw the big, heavy lures weighing from 1 to 3½ ounces, and to withstand the gruelling battles with big fish, battles that sometimes last as long as three hours. A rod with backbone is also necessary to work the big lures properly, to give the action that will pop a large bug, pull it under the water for a foot or a yard, which maneuver sets up bursting bubbles and makes the water roil around the plug, a sure way to interest hungry game fish. Similarly, the strong tip is necessary when going deep, to "jig" a heavy lure up and down, again a very great attractor for some of these ocean-going heavyweights; and to lift big fish in a way not possible with the more elastic spinning rod.

These rods are equipped with the heavy-duty plug-casting reels mentioned earlier, fitted with a cub drag that allows the angler to fight a fish to the limit of his knowledge. He can adjust the drag to the point where a bit more strain would result in a snapped line, or a bit less would give the fish too much leeway and prolong the battle endlessly. He has control of his own game.

Two hundred yards of 15-pound test monofilament line is fairly standard lining for the plug-casting outfit, and leaders are generally made of ✳5 or ✳6 wire attached to the line with a swivel in order to prevent twisting. In conformity with the regulations of most sportfishing contests, plugcasters usually limit the length of the leader to the length of the rod tip.

Most users of this heavy gear always go equipped with extra line. Although monofilament can withstand the pull of really big fish to an amazing degree, occasionally a fish will hit and just never stop, taking all the line. And when it hits the knot where it is tied to the reel core there is a "tick" and off goes the fish, trailing behind him a 200-yard-long tail. Sometimes, too, a big horse of a fish will dive and cut the line on rocks below. So take plenty of extra line with you when you go out with the big outfit.

This also applies to lures. On one Panama trip we lost three dozen plugs. Another time we lost 130 in four days to fish that hit and dived and cut us off. But it was so much fun that we stayed with them to the bitter end, until they cleaned us out.

Both surface and underwater plugs are popular because some fish, such as the groupers, are deep dwellers, which you must reach by going down with heavy jigs, while others, such as the snappers, may occasionally be taken in relatively shallow water on surface poppers. Similarly, some of the more exotic catches, such as the Pacific sailfish and the high-leaping dolphin, are surface swimmers.

Therefore lures range from popping plugs and surface runners to others that work several feet beneath the surface, and the selection is rounded out with lead-headed jigs designed to go down to the farthest depths. The lures are large in size, some as much as 7 inches, and they are weighty, going from 1½ to 3½ ounces. They are fitted with hooks in sizes from 1/0 to 3/0 and in the case of some of the big jigs the hooks go as high as 5/0.

Most plugs are fitted with two or three sets of treble hooks and many manufacturers join these together with heavy wire inside the plug. Failing this, the angler who has done much of this type of fishing soon learns to wire them together himself. It is nothing for these big fish to pull out or smash one set of gang hooks, and with the added wire the second set is then a safeguard against losing the quarry.

Casting with the heavy plugging outfit is not difficult but it takes a bit of practice for accuracy. And you soon learn not to try to cast directly into the wind, because those big lures offer so much resistance that the reel is almost sure to overspin. The main thing to remember is always to look in back of you before you cast, just as surf casters do, so that you will not hook anything or any person, with the wide-arm swing required.

This is particularly important since for this type of fishing you are frequently fishing from a charter boat, with consequently limited space. On one trip to Panama, Luke Gorham, Moses Nunnally, and I worked out a good system so that the three of us could fish continuously. Luke would start on the left side of the cockpit, while I would take up my position on the right side, casting aft, with Moses standing right behind me.

I would get off a right-handed cast, then immediately move over to the center of the cockpit to play my lure, while Moses would step into the spot I had just vacated, make his cast, and play his lure. Meantime, Luke would make his throw backhand and play his lure in. Then he would move over behind Moses.

I would keep going to the left and take up the position Luke had just quitted. It was a constant circle, except, of course, when the rhythm was shattered by strikes and fights with fish, as when one man would get into a particularly tough fish and the other two would have to bring in their lures and wait out the fight. Sometimes two of us would have fish on at the same time and a couple of times we hooked triple headers and then the manipulation of rods and lines was something to see.

In the following pictures, Luke Gorham, president of the Metropolitan Miami Fishing Tournament, and crack Miami Beach Rod and Reel Club angler, who has long been an exponent of the art of heavy plug casting, demonstrates his technique.

THE RIGHT-HAND CAST

The grip for the conventional right-hand cast is much like that used by golfers, the right hand with forefinger hooked over the finger grip of the rod, the other fingers coming around and up on the cork, and the thumb resting on the line on the spool. The left hand grasps the cork with thumb on top and fingers going around under the grip. This

PICTURE NO. 39

PICTURE NO. 40

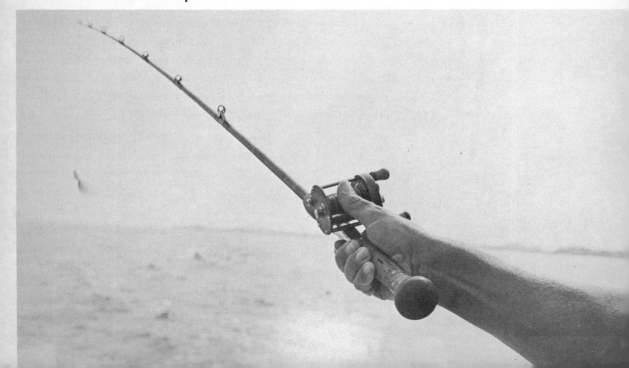

gives a steady, firm hold, as shown in picture No. 39, and allows the angler to go into the wide-arm casting motion without the rod slipping in his hands.

Because the cast is made with a swing and with a much slower wrist snap than used in light plug casting, the lure is dropped about 18 inches below the tip of the rod, as shown in picture No. 40. This allows it to follow the rod around and shoot straight out when the

PICTURE NO. 41

PICTURE NO. 42

113

angler releases the line, and achieves greater distance and more accuracy than if the heavy lure were held close to the rod tip.

The cast is begun with the rod thrust backward, as in picture No. 41, the left arm held straight, as in golf, the left wrist cocked for the throw. Picture No. 42 reveals that Luke uses a typical open stance used by golfers, as he brings the rod back ready for the throw.

In picture No. 43 he has started the cast. Notice how the plug is pulled along by the rod tip. At this moment, the wrists have not yet gone into action. But as the rod comes up, Luke gets his wrists into the cast, with a smooth but strong snap, and follows through with the right wrist turning over so the reel handles are up and spinning freely. As shown in picture No. 44, the follow-through is so definite that he has risen slightly on his toes.

At the end of the throw the arms are extended and the right wrist is well over, as shown in picture No. 45. The plug is beginning to drop to the water, and the whirling reel handles are slowing. Picture

PICTURE NO. 43

No. 46 shows how the rod is held straight out toward the point where the angler wishes the plug to hit. If it should seem to be going to overshoot the mark, the caster can slow it down by thumbing the reel.

The plug has now hit the water and Luke is ready for the retrieve. As shown in picture No. 47, the rod is held well up to withstand a heavy strike, and the left side of the reel is pressed in against the inside of Luke's left wrist for steadiness, a big help in fighting a fish.

Picture No. 48 shows the firm grasp on the foregrip of the rod and how the butt is shoved back securely just below the belt, for a firm

PICTURE NO. 44

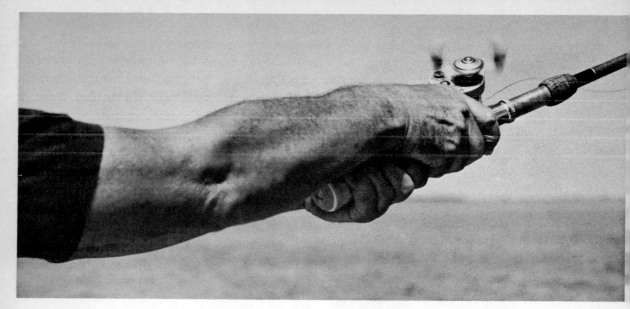

PICTURE NO. 46

116

base during the retrieve. Many anglers use a belt cup for rod butt placement, and this is a very comfortable addition to the gear when you are fighting a big fish for a long time.

From this position the rod can be brought up and back sharply for a strike, as shown in picture No. 49.

With a fish on and running, the angler grasps one reel knob firmly between thumb and forefinger, and extends the other fingers of the right hand to steady the other knob, as shown in picture No. 50, so

PICTURE NO. 47

PICTURE NO. 48

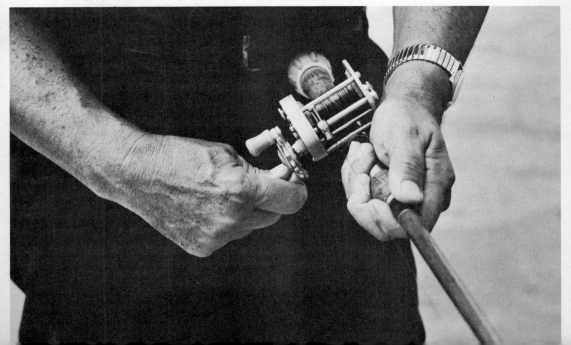

that the reel handle cannot spin. The fish is now pulling against the cub drag. Left thumb lightly rests on line, ready for a quick push down if more drag is required.

Picture No. 51 again shows how the fingers of the right hand control both reel grips.

When the fish has settled down to a steady fight, the angler gets settled too. The thumb goes up to the top of the reel, ready to be placed on the reel spool to add pressure to that of the preset cub

PICTURE NO. 49

PICTURE NO. 50

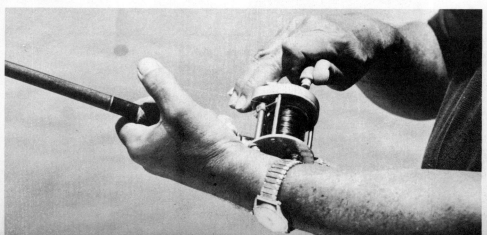

118

drag, if necessary. All four fingers cup the reel firmly, reaching up on the right side to hold the one reel handle tightly, while the other handle rests against the first finger, as shown in picture No. 52. Thus the handles are locked securely, so they cannot spin. The left thumb, pressing lightly on the line as it comes off the reel, can also apply pressure if need be.

If the fish makes a run, both thumbs are lifted, while the fingers of the right hand continue to hold the reel handles fixed, as the fish peels off line against the power of the cub drag.

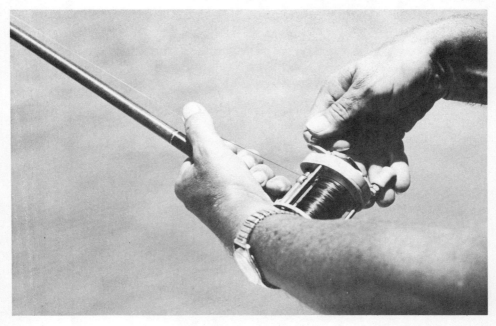

PICTURE NO. 51

PICTURE NO. 52

119

THE BACKHAND CAST

There are many times when an angler does not have room for the right-hand cast—as for instance the incident described in the introduction to this chapter, when Luke Gorham, Moses Nunnally, and I were fishing from the cockpit of a charter boat. The man on the right side can make a right-hand cast, but the one on the left must make his throw backhand.

To do this, the right hand takes the same grip as for the conventional right-hand cast, forefinger hooked over the finger grip, and thumb on the line spool. But the left hand moves forward as shown in picture No. 53, ahead of the reel, around the foregrip of the rod. Now the left elbow is pulled in and the right arm extended

PICTURE NO. 53

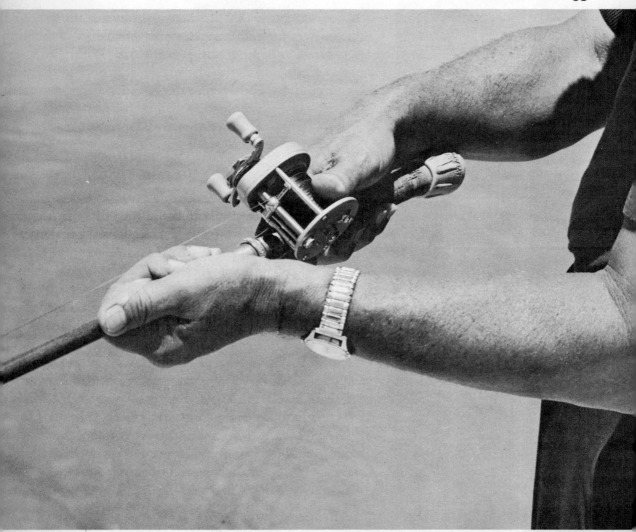

121

as shown in picture No. 54, straight back to the left, ready to start the cast.

As in the right-hand cast, the throw is made with a slight lifting loop, which gives the lure an upward slant to achieve more distance than a lower trajectory would give. Picture No. 55 shows the rod at the top of the lift, line shooting up and out. And picture No. 56 shows the same position from above, as the reel handles slow and the lure drops to the surface.

PICTURE NO. 56

An assortment of heavy plug-casting lures—big surface poppers, underwater swimmers, and deep-riding jigs. Left side of the rod, top to bottom:
Creek Chub popping plug, Leaping Lena, Creek Chub popper, Upperman ⧓9 bucktail. Right side of rod, top to bottom: Tightline lure, Upperman Big Ben.
Typical outfit used by the heavy plugcaster. Note the size of the plug, dwarfing the angler's hand, in picture No. 58.

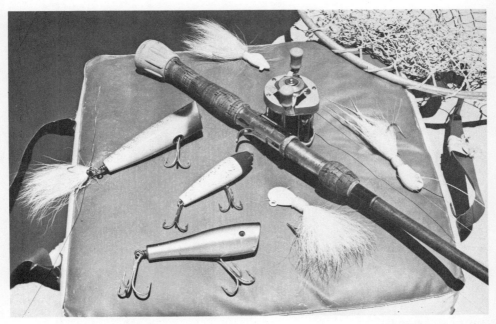

PICTURE NO. 57

PICTURE NO. 58

PART III
SPINNING

CHAPTER 6   HOW TO SPIN CAST

INTRODUCTION

Across the big Norwegian salmon river I saw a man twirl a line around his head, the big silver spoon on the end of it flashing in the sun. As it came around on the sixth twirl, he released the line and the spoon shot out over the river. Now he shoved the bright tin can that he held in his other hand out after the moving line.

"What is he doing?" I asked.

"He's a tin-can fisherman," my gillie replied. "He has his line wrapped around a smooth tin can and when he throws the big spoon out, it pulls the line off the tin after it—he's casting."

"The same idea as a fixed spool," I said. "How long has this been going on."

"For as long as there have been tin cans," the gillie replied.

A year later, far down in Patagonia, I saw an Argentine wood chopper fishing in exactly the same manner except that instead of the can he used an empty wine bottle as the fixed spool.

Fifteen thousand miles apart and probably neither of these fishermen had ever heard of spinning, yet they were using the same basic principle as the spinning reels which have taken the United States by storm in the past fifteen years.

It's true that spinning was practiced in Europe for better than a century before it achieved any popularity or even notice in the United States. In 1945 there were less than a couple of hundred spin fishermen on this continent—and by 1950 it seemed that spinning would clear the decks of every other kind of light-tackle fishing. The converts to spinning were so vociferous, so loud in their praises, and so successful in their fishing that for a while it looked as if all other methods would go by the boards.

For one thing, a rank beginner could pick up a spinning outfit—or so it happened on occasion—and cast 50 feet on the first try, and catch fish. The thin monofilament line was so nearly invisible that fish hit much more readily than they did on the heavier plug-casting lines. And because of the distance that even a neophyte could cast, even with a light, ⅛-ounce lure, he could reach out farther than the fly fisherman.

In time it evolved that these apparent advantages were not necessarily the solution to all casting needs, and once that was discovered spinning settled down in its own place in the angling field, and plug and fly casting returned to theirs. Today many flycasters and plugcasters who formerly looked on spinning with a degree of bitterness have come to realize that this method of casting has been the means of attracting great numbers of people to the sport of fishing, simply because of the ease with which it could be learned; and from there they have gone on to the other methods of fishing.

But it is something of a misstatement to say that spinning is easy. Like every other kind of sport, it has its pitfalls and it has its tricks, and the beginner will learn faster and more easily if he knows how to avoid the one and take advantage of the other.

His first step should be to learn exactly what kind of spinning equipment he should have for the kind of fishing he intends to do. For, like plug- and fly-casting outfits, spinning rods, reels, and lures should be adjusted to the occasion in order that the caster may obtain the most enjoyment and the greatest success from his sport.

Fresh-water spinning, for instance, calls for a 5½- to 6½-foot rod weighing 4 or 5 ounces, and the reel need hold only 185 to 225 yards (more if the angler wishes, of course,) of 4- or 6-pound test monofilament line. While some sweet-water spinners insist on using heavier line, 8-pound test or even 10-pound test, they would have more success in casting and would get more strikes with a lighter line. And the lighter lines will handle any fish that is likely to be encountered in fresh water, with the possible exception of big northern pike, muskies, or very large trout or Atlantic salmon in extremely heavy water.

Salt-water spinning generally demands a heavier outfit. Here, a 6½- to 7-foot medium action rod weighing 5 to 7 ounces, and a reel that will hold 400 yards of 6- or 8-pound test monofilament are sufficient for the smaller salt-water species. But for heavier species and when fishing from the shore, fishing at night, or casting over the reefs, a 7½- to 8½-foot rod is often used, weighing 7 to 12 ounces. With this, salt-water spinners use a big reel capable of holding 400 yards of 10- or 12-pound test line, for in such fishing you never really know with what species you may tangle.

In salt-water spinning a heavier strand of nylon is also often used to form an 18-inch trace next to the lure, and some anglers go as high as 20-pounds test for this trace. For fish that have extra-long and sharp teeth, such as the barracuda, bluefish, and mackerel, a wire leader is in order.

Like the expert plugcaster, the expert spinner chooses his rod to fit the lure he will be casting. Ideally, he would carry about five rods with him in order to be able to have the proper stick for the plug he wishes to use. But the average spin caster can readily circumvent this problem by a simple adjustment of the distance of the lure from the rod tip when he makes his cast. The lighter the lure, the farther it should hang down from the rod tip.

For instance, with a medium-weight spinning rod, which is what the average fisherman will have, a ⅜-ounce lure should hang down less than a foot from the rod tip. With the same rod, a ¼-ounce jig-type lure would be dropped to 15 inches below the rod tip, and a ⅛-ounce lure would be dropped a good 2 feet. Timing is very important with the longer distance between rod tip and lure and so is care to avoid catching a fellow angler, but there is no doubt that both ease in casting and distance achieved are greatly enhanced.

Spinning is versatile, too. The angler may cast light plugs, heavy plugs, spoons, and jigs, and he may also cast much more delicate temptations to fish. Many trout fishermen, finding that the big, heavy lures frighten fish in a still pool or when they are rising exclusively to a hatch, use a floating bubble with fly attached to the leader. The bubble provides the casting weight necessary and the fly deceives the wary fish. A spinning outfit also allows the bait fisherman to cast a gob of worms, a live minnow, or a live shrimp, lightly and easily without a heavy sinker to announce its arrival with a big splash.

Since the first European spinning reels came to the U.S.A. there have been a great many changes and improvements made. A strictly American innovation in the field is the enclosed-type spinning reel now being widely used, especially in fresh water. In the following pictures three different reels have been used in order to illustrate the essential differences in handling of the different types. But regardless of the reel, when it comes to casting, certain basic techniques apply. In the wide expanse of lakes or salt seas there is seldom any need for anything but the straight overhead cast. But when you fish the shore lines, sheltered coves, shady streams, and when you run into some of nature's hazards, such as wind, there are a number of special casts that the angler can call on to get him into or out of a tight spot and put more fish in his creel.

In the following pictures the important basic casts, plus some of the more exotic ones, are demonstrated by Gordon Dean of the famous sporting-goods house of Abercrombie & Fitch, of New York City. He was one of the earliest proponents of spinning and an expert in both fresh and salt water.

THE GRIP

The open-face spinning reel is set on the reel seat under the rod, so that the reel is down when casting. With this type of reel, Gordon Dean finds that he gets the most comfortable hold when he places two fingers on each side of the leg by which the reel is attached to the rod. In picture No. 1 he shows how to spread the fingers, first and second finger forward of the reel leg, third and little finger to the rear of it. The spread fingers are then slid under the grip, as shown in picture No. 2, and go on in until the reel leg stops the forward shove.

PICTURE NO. 1

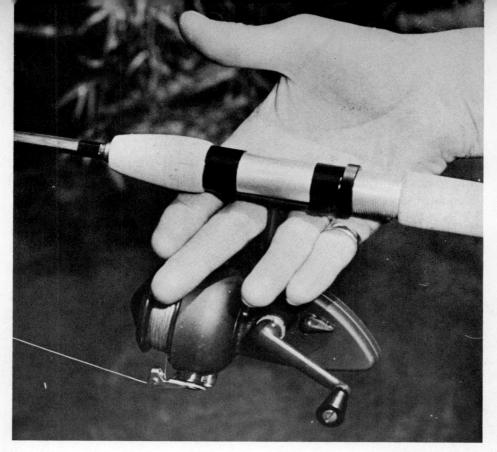

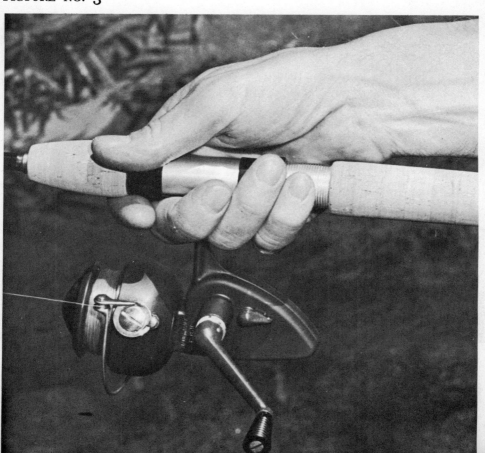

Now the fingers close around the rod in a natural grip, loose but firm and comfortable. Then the thumb is brought over to lie just a little to the left of the top of the rod grip. As seen in picture No. 3, this is much like gripping a golf club with the right hand.

With the American enclosed-type spinning reels, however, Gordon finds that the most comfortable grip is as shown in picture No. 4, hand and wrist forward of the reel and above it, allowing easy wrist movement and, again, the thumb lies over slightly to the left.

PICTURE NO. 4

LINE CONTROL

Since the spinning reel must be in free spool in order to cast, there must be some control of the line to prevent the lure from pulling out until the moment when the caster wishes to release it.

With the bail-type reel, the line is picked up with the forefinger of the right hand, just above the reel. Then the bail is pushed for-

PICTURE NO. 5

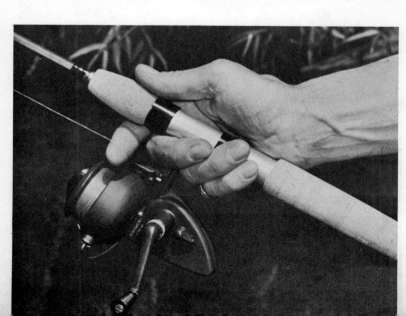

PICTURE NO. 6

133

ward and down, as shown in picture No. 5, until it stops and holds. Now, with the finger controlling the line, the angler is ready to cast, as shown in picture No. 6.

Because they believe there is less chance of mechanical failure, many fishermen prefer the spinning reel which does not have a bail (called the manual pickup) or any other form of automatic

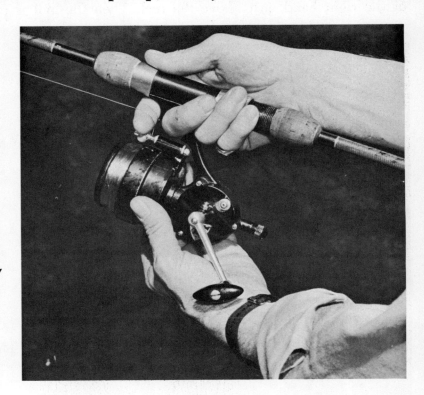

PICTURE NO. 7

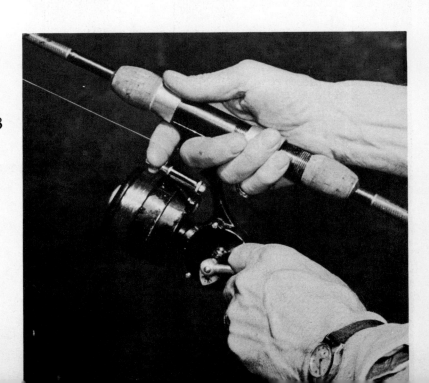

PICTURE NO. 8

PICTURE NO. 9

PICTURE NO. 10

135

pickup. With such reels, the knob of the reel is brought around to the position shown in picture No. 7, so the forefinger of the casting hand can reach out and pick up the line.

Now, with the line hooked over the forefinger, Gordon turns the reel handle, as shown in picture No. 8, so that the knob moves down under the reel, out of the way of the line. And in picture No. 9 he is ready to cast. The knob is at the bottom of the reel, the line running direct from reel to finger.

The method of controlling line that Gordon Dean recommends when using a closed-face reel is shown in picture No. 10. The left hand picks up the line about 6 inches in front of the reel and brings it up and around the back of the hand, then lays it against the rod grip, where the right thumb then presses down, to hold the line until he wishes to let the lure start out. Then, as shown in picture No. 11, a touch on the push button on the back of the reel puts it in free spool and he is ready to cast.

PICTURE NO. 11

THE STRAIGHTAWAY CAST

Once the angler has mastered the mechanical differences in the various types of spinning reels, the casts are much the same for all of them and throughout the following series Gordon Dean has used all three types of reels.

Ninety per cent of the time, the spin fisherman will be using a simple, straightaway cast and this is the throw he should learn thor-

PICTURE NO. 12

oughly before he moves on to anything else, so he can cast accurately for long as well as short distances. Once he is proficient at the straight-away cast, the others will follow easily.

In picture No. 12, Gordon sights his target along a line between his eye and the lowest rod guide. Then with a quick flip of the wrist he brings the rod back in a straight up and down groove, as shown in picture No. 13, and stops the rod at the two o'clock position. Note that the arm hardly enters into the cast at all. From

PICTURE NO. 13

this position, a good, quick forward flip of the wrist will impart a decided bend to the rod, supplying the necessary spring for the forward cast. To show the proper position, Gordon has stopped the rod, but in actual casting there is no appreciable pause at the peak of the backcast. It is a quick backward flip of the wrist, and immediately a quick forward flip of the wrist.

At the moment when he wishes to release the line and let the lure head on out toward the target, Gordon raises his thumb where it

PICTURE NO. 14

has been pressing the line tight against the grip, and stops the rod at the ten o'clock position, as shown in picture No. 14.

However, if casting into the wind, he brings the rod tip down smartly, as shown in picture No. 15, releasing the lure at the ten o'clock position but continuing the rod on down in a hard follow-through that keeps the lure down low, under the wind. This is very important because a cast which is finished high, even in a moderate

PICTURE NO. 15

breeze, may cost the angler considerable distance, especially if he is using a large, wind-resistant lure or surface plug.

On the other hand, if a strong wind is blowing from behind him, he may get comparable extra distance by extending the arm slightly as he makes the forward flip of the wrist, and stopping the rod high, as shown in picture No. 16. Such a cast can add yards to the throw, but does not achieve quite the accuracy of the regular cast.

PICTURE NO. 16

HOW TO STOP THE LURE

In the course of the day's fishing, the angler may frequently over-shoot his mark or for some other reason may wish to stop the lure before it stops of its own momentum. Sometimes the cast may have been made too hard, so the lure is going beyond where he wishes it to land, or up into bushes on the far side of a stream. Again, he may see a rising fish in some direction other than the one in which he has cast and he may want to stop the lure quickly so he can reel in and throw to that riser.

PICTURE NO. 17

The simplest method of stopping the lure is to push forward on the reel handle with the left hand, as shown in picture No. 17, thus putting the reel into gear and stopping the lure in mid-air. This method is usually used when speed is essential in halting the lure before it flies wildly into bushes. It is quick and simple.

But there are many circumstances where a less sudden stop, a little more finesse, and a little more control are required. In picture No. 18 Gordon shows how the outgoing line may be stopped whenever the angler chooses by hooking the index finger under it. Note that this is the same position from which the line was originally released.

PICTURE NO. 18

A third method, illustrated in picture No. 19, shows how the angler may achieve still more control. By pressing the finger lightly or heavily, or alternately lightly and heavily, against the reel spool, he can slow the cast down, let it go again, slow it again, or stop it, as he pleases. This takes skill, and consequently it takes practice, but in time a very complete control of the cast can be achieved.

PICTURE NO. 19

THE SIDEARM CAST

The sidearm cast is especially useful when wading a stream or in any similar spot where overhanging branches or bushes prevent the use of the straightaway overhead cast. It is also a very good cast to use in the wind as it keeps the lure on a low level throughout the throw.

The sidearm cast is started as shown in picture No. 20, with the rod held out in front, elbow bent, rod tip slanting down slightly below the parallel with the water. Then the rod tip is brought back to the side, on the same plane and using wrist movement entirely. Picture No. 21 shows how this short backthrust of the wrist will keep the rod in an arc close to the caster, whereas a wide-arm-movement cast would allow a much wider arc with more room in which to go off on the timing and perhaps release the lure so it would shoot out to the side instead of straight ahead.

In picture No. 22 the angler completes the cast with a snap of the wrist, again on the same plane, releasing the lure as it comes around to the target.

PICTURE NO. 20

THE BACKHAND CAST

When background objects prevent either a straightaway or a sidearm cast, the angler can often get himself out of a tight spot by using a backhand cast. In picture No. 23 Gordon Dean shows the starting position. The lure is allowed to hang down from the rod tip at least 12 inches, and the hand comes around on the grip, to the left, for easier wrist action. Note that now and throughout this cast the reel handles are down.

In picture No. 24 Gordon brings the rod back across his left shoulder, pointed slightly above the parallel. Then the arm is brought slowly forward from the elbow. As the lure approaches the target, the wrist is snapped through with good force, the line is released, and the caster follows through with the arm, as shown in picture No. 25, finishing at a point well out in front and slightly higher than his head.

PICTURE NO. 23

148

THE FLIP CAST

Like the sidearm cast, the flip cast is most useful when the angler
is fishing a small, brushy river or when deep water crowds him
against a brush-filled or steep bank that does not allow room for free
use of the rod. The most important thing to remember with this cast
is that the lure must be held tight against, or at most not more than
an inch from, the rod tip. With lure in that position, in picture No. 26,
Gordon Dean extends the rod out in front as he would for the regular
straightaway cast.

As the name suggests, the cast is executed entirely by a flip of the
wrist. To get a strong forward flip, the rod tip must be brought down
to the water with a hard downward thrust, which, in turn, will put

PICTURE NO. 26

PICTURE NO. 27

PICTURE NO. 28

150

a good bend in the tip when the forward throw is started. Picture No. 27 shows how the downward push followed by the hard forward flip of the wrist puts a good solid bend in the rod.

As shown in picture No. 28, as the rod straightens out it flips the lure forward. For a short cast, Gordon will release the line from under his thumb at this moment, allowing the lure to go out. For a longer cast, he will carry the rod on up, as shown in picture No. 29, releasing the line at a higher level so the lure will soar upward as well as forward, and thus achieve more distance.

PICTURE NO. 29

THE GRASSHOPPER CAST

Many a time a spin caster spots a deep dark hole back under trees or bushes or under an overhanging bank where it is almost impossible to place a lure by a regular cast. This is the place for the "grasshopper," a throw that is designed to make the lure hit the water a foot or so in front of the opening, in a spot which is clear of obstructions, and then hop into the danger zone where a big fish probably lurks.

To execute the grasshopper cast, Gordon crouches low, holding his rod slightly to the side at a 40-degree angle. He has reeled the lure in until it is barely 6 inches from the rod tip. Now he brings the rod back with wrist movement only, to the angle shown in picture No. 30.

PICTURE NO. 30

This photograph shows the rod stopped at the end of the backward movement, but in the cast there is actually no noticeable pause between backward movement and forward throw.

Now he brings the rod forward smartly on a flat plane, with rod tip parallel to the water. Just before releasing the line he gives a hard push to the rod tip. Picture No. 31 shows the position of the rod as it sends the lure out on a low trajectory so that it hits the water a glancing blow. The water disturbance in the center of the photo marks the spot where the lure first hit, and against the right-hand edge the further disturbances show its second hop as it skidded under the bank like a stone that has been skipped across the surface.

PICTURE NO. 31

THE UNDERHAND LOB

The underhand lob is a valuable cast in confined water or where the fish are scary. It is made without any hard downward throw and therefore allows the caster to drop the lure with a minimum of splash. To execute the underhand lob, the rod is held out to the right, slightly above the parallel to the water, and with the lure hanging about 24 inches below the tip, as shown in picture No. 32. The hand is rolled around to the right side, rather than lying on top of the grip. Thus, when the rod is brought back in the backcast, using wrist action only, as shown in picture No. 33, note how the whole hand is under the grip.

Now the caster comes forward easily and without imparting any push to the cast, and still maintaining the hand position. He releases the lure at his target, allowing it to go out in a slow arc, then continues the rod tip on up to about the two o'clock position, as shown in picture No. 34. The lure will enter the water with a minimum of splash.

PICTURE NO. 32

PICTURE NO. 33

PICTURE NO. 34

THE BACKHAND LOB CAST

The backhand lob cast is useful when a steep bank or trees in back of him prevent the regular forward cast, and the angler wants to drop his lure with the least possible noise.

Gordon Dean starts the backhand lob as shown in picture No. 35, with rod held out so the tip lies a little below the parallel to the water. The lure is dropped 12 to 18 inches below the tip. He comes back with the rod across his body, well below the left shoulder, elbow high, as shown in picture No. 36, so that the rod tip is down and the lure just clears the ground or water, as the case may be, as it is brought back.

Then he comes forward with a sweep of the rod, imparting a good snap to the wrist and releasing the line as he approaches the target. Then he carries the rod on up as shown in picture No. 37. As with the regular lob cast, the lure will fall with very little noise or splash.

PICTURE NO. 35

THE BOW AND ARROW CAST

The bow and arrow cast is often referred to as a trick cast, but there are many times when it will get the angler out of a tight spot, and with a little practice it is easy to do. However, considerable care should be taken in handling the lure, as the bowed rod has a great deal of force and it is easy to make a slip and sink the hooks into the fingers. With the lure pictured here, the angler holds the plug by its tail feathers and well back of the hooks, which are placed in the middle of

PICTURE NO. 38

the lure. If there are no feathers or bucktail, the lure should be held by the bend of the hook, or hooks, if treble ones.

With right arm thrust well out in front, Gordon pulls back hard on the lure, thus giving the rod a good bow, as shown in picture No. 38. His right thumb holds the line tight against the rod grip. From this position he will give a short, hard forward flip of his right wrist and release the lure at the peak of the force. As the rod snaps through, he lifts his finger from the line and both lure and line will shoot on out.

When tree limbs overhead prevent the regular bow and arrow cast, the same cast may be made in reverse, under the rod, as it were, as illustrated in picture No. 39, with rod and lure held low rather than overhead. When the cast is made from this angle, the lure achieves much the same trajectory as in the flip cast.

PICTURE NO. 39

THE RETRIEVE

Varying weights and construction of lures and varying depths of water call for different ways of handling the retrieve of a spinning lure, but a good general rule is that the rod should always be high enough, as shown in picture No. 40, that it can absorb the shock of a sudden

PICTURE NO. 40

hit from a fish, rather than so low that the pull will go straight to the reel, which might snap the line.

From this position the angler can readily put the force of his body into a good solid strike to hook the fish, as shown in picture No. 41.

When retrieving a lure in very shallow water or working the pockets

in back of rocks with a lure that weighs more than ¼ ounce, the rod may be held much higher. Gordon Dean illustrates this in picture No. 42, reaching as high as possible so that the lure will swim freely through the shallow places and will be at such an angle that it will skid over rocks that may lie just under the surface. A fast retrieve will still further accentuate this high-riding tendency.

PICTURE NO. 42

PART IV
FISHING THE SURF

CHAPTER 7   HOW TO SURF CAST

INTRODUCTION

Surf casting is as old as the Union. Immediately after the Civil War, "bassing clubs" were common among well-to-do sportsmen in New York and throughout New England. These old-timers did their surf casting in high style. Platforms were erected along suitable shores in good striped-bass waters and from these stands hired "chummers" tossed overboard a wide variety of foodstuffs to tempt the great schools of fish within range. Beside them the doughty anglers stood at the ready, to heave out their baits and snag a passing behemoth lured in by the proffered smorgasbord.

A shortage of bass about the turn of the century caused the clubs to disband and surf casting was carried on only as a spotty sport, by an unhonored few. But the bass began to come back and so did the surf casters. From New England down through Maryland, Delaware, North and South Carolina, and on to Florida, as well as increasingly on the west coast of the United States, surf casters sought the striped bass and began to turn to other species as well. The channel bass, kingfish, weakfish, spotted weakfish, shore-running species such as the jacks—you never knew what you might hook in the surf but it was fun to find out, and the numbers of followers of this type of fishing grew.

Surf-fishing areas are by nature remote, lonely, difficult to reach, usually rough as to terrain and weather. Surf fishing requires a certain type of fisherman, one who revels in the riotous breakers, in the bleak beauty of the sandy wastes of Cape Cod and Hatteras, the austere expanses of endless ocean beyond the surf. He must be independent, self-reliant, and rugged. He must belong to the sea. It follows that one of the spots where surf casting has reached its highest development is Cape Cod, Massachusetts, always the home of seafaring folks and today the favorite fishing territory of the members of the Massachusetts Beach Buggy Association.

When the word goes out that the fish are in, a strange stream of odd contraptions pours out of Boston, Worcester, Providence, and all the neighboring communities, a stream of "beach buggies," ingeniously built around trucks, jeeps, and revved-up cars of various kinds, all powered and wheeled to drive the deep sand beaches and equipped to operate for periods of several days without contact with civilization. Each carries its own fresh water and food. Cooking and sleeping facilities are built into the buggies. Many are equipped with boats.

Out on the beach the surf caster lives in a world apart. Fishing goes on around the clock, each man working according to his own opinion of when the fish hit best. There's always someone fishing and someone sleeping and someone else with a pot of coffee on the stove and a yarn to spin. Many women are surf casters, too, and children are initiated young, equipped with "chokem" plugs to cast along the sand. The name is derived from the parents' admonition that, while there isn't any hook on the plugs, should a fish hit one it will choke to death on it. As these tyros grow up, they graduate to plugs with lead over the hooks so they will not hook themselves; and by the time a beach-buggy kid is big enough to look after himself, you can bet he's a first-rate surf caster.

Like devotees of the other branches of casting, surf casters have developed highly efficient gear for their sport. Rods may be of hollow glass, split bamboo, or natural cane and may be either one- or two-piece, with a minimum of three guides plus the tip guide. These surf rods are built with three different kinds of action, each designed for certain line tests. There is the light squidding rod, 8 to 8½ feet in length, with whippy action designed to toss small lures and squids in the 1½- to 2-ounce bracket, on line running from 25- to 36-pound test. For a lure weighing from 2 to 3½ ounces and a line in the 36- to 45-pound test class, the standard Atlantic surf rod is a medium-weight stick measuring 9 to 9½ feet in length. And for extra-long casts and extra-heavy duty such as is often required at Cape Cod and along the North Carolina Outer Banks, surf casters usually advocate a 10- or 11-foot powerhouse of a rod, designed for just one thing—to throw a 3- to 5-ounce lure a long way. This rod handles 36- to 45-pound test line.

The old-time surf line was made of linen but today's big reels are lined almost entirely with nylon monofilament, nylon braid, or, occasionally, dacron. In high-surf areas where big fish are taken, nylon braid is the most popular.

There is also a variation of the standard rod called a "jetty stick," used for snap casting from rocks where heavy waves wash in, or in spots where there is no room for a backward shove of the rod, as in the regular cast. This jetty stick is usually about 2 feet long in the butt with the tip running 5½ to 6 feet. It is a handy rod when casting from a boat, too, especially if the caster must work from a sitting position.

The surf casting reel must be light, strong, free-spooling, and have a smooth star drag. The gear ratio is approximately 3½ to 1, and spool capacity varies from 150 to 200 yards of 36-pound test line. Veteran casters prefer the wide spool because it is easier to lay the line on smoothly and symmetrically, one of the most important considerations in surf casting, since a bunched-up line will not cast well and middle-of-the-reel humps can result in some fantastic backlashes.

Spinning has also invaded the surf and there are two popular rods in this field. One is a 7½-foot stick, from butt to tip, used to cast lures in the ½- to 1½-ounce range, and equipped with 6- to 8-pound test monofilament; the other, designed to handle midget plugs and small squids, measures 8 to 9 feet in length and handles 8- to 10-pound test line. With this one, you can throw a lure weighing from ¾ to 2 ounces. Some few surf fishermen go for an even heavier spinning outfit when looking for extra-big fish, a rod that will handle 12- or 15-pound test line and throw big lures weighing 3 and 4 ounces. The big spinning reels carry 200 to 250 yards of line, usually monofilament.

Surf casters use all varieties of lures. There are surface popping plugs, underwater swimming plugs, spoons, jigs, and eelskin and squid combinations. For natural bait they turn to squid, sea clams, or skinmers, sand eels, and many kinds of baitfish and cut bait. At any given time, the local tackle store in an area where surf fishing is good will have something to recommend as "what they're taking now," and it will usually be right.

All this big, stout, highly specialized tackle takes considerable handling and in the following pictures, two of the country's top surf casters are pictured showing how it's done. Hal Lyman, publisher of the *Salt Water Sportsman* magazine, handles the regular surf reel. Frank Woolner, editor of the same magazine, shows how to spin the surf.

ROD POSITION FOR SURF CASTING

A comfortable position for both hand and arm is essential when using the big surf casting outfit. In picture No. 1, Hal Lyman shows the perfect fitting rod . . . when the butt is set tight into the armpit and the rod held straight out, his thumb rests comfortably on the reel spool, without reaching or strain.

PICTURE NO. 1

Preparatory to casting, the rod is gripped as shown in picture No. 2, with the right hand well up on the cork back of the reel so that the hand fits snugly around the grip and the thumb rests lightly on the line on the spool. The left hand holds the butt of the rod, either a few inches from the end or, as is surf caster Lyman's preference, right at the end. This lower hand position is a matter of choice, depending on which grip feels most comfortable to the individual.

PICTURE NO. 2

ADJUSTMENT OF THE DRAG

In case a fish should hit as soon as the lure or bait lands, the drag is set before a cast is made. Many fish are lost through faulty drag adjustment. A loose drag makes it almost impossible to set the hook hard enough to sink the barb. But a too-heavy drag may result in a broken line on the strike, or may cause the hook to pull out. Most experienced surfmen find it wise to err on the light side, using just enough pressure to prevent overspin but still enough to hold the fish back when he runs.

PICTURE NO. 3

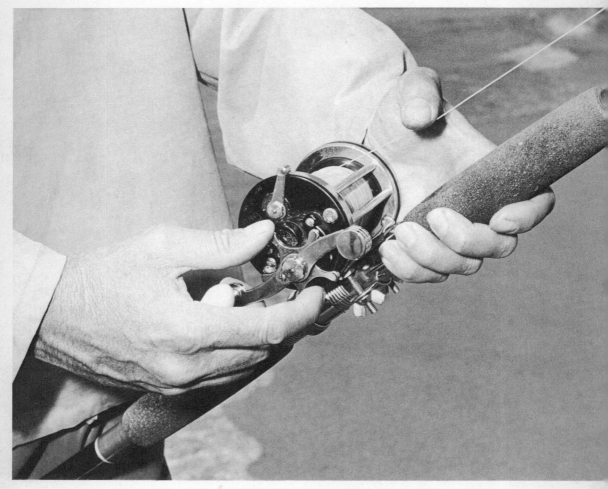

Reels vary in design, but drag adjustment is usually made by a simple twist of the star drag as shown in picture No. 3. After a fish has hit and settled down in his fight, the angler can readily readjust this to set the drag to fit the struggles and size of the fish.

The strength of line being used must always be considered, too, and personal judgment enters greatly into the picture. In picture No. 4, Hal Lyman tests the drag adjustment he has made by means of strong, smooth pulls upward from the reel to see if he thinks it will stand the force of a strike, yet give to the sudden surges of a big fish.

PICTURE NO. 4

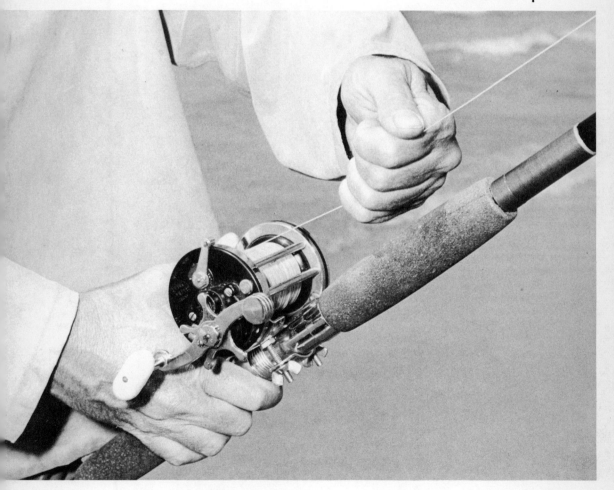

HOW TO PUT THE REEL IN FREE SPOOL

So that line can peel out easily, the surf-casting reel must be in "free spool" when the cast is made. To hold the line tight during the cast, up to the moment when he wishes to let it go out, the caster uses the thumb of his right hand to apply pressure to the line on the spool, as shown in picture No. 5, while the left thumb pushes the handle that releases the spool. Release handle may move either forward or backward, depending on the design of the reel.

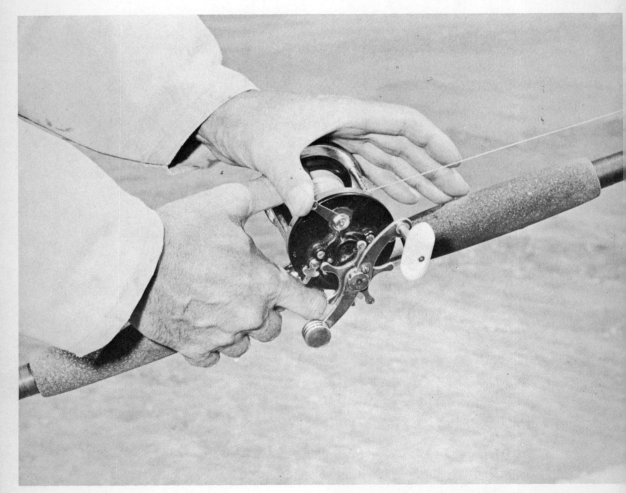

PICTURE NO. 5

THUMBING THE REEL

Most casters keep the right thumb lightly pressed against the line at the middle of the reel core throughout the cast, as shown in picture No. 6. Others remove the pressure once the forward movement is begun, but this is a step only for the expert, because, while the removal of the thumb pressure, however light, allows more speed and distance, it also tends to let the spool overspin, with resultant bird's nest.

Another way to thumb the line is shown in picture No. 7, where the thumb lies against the side of the spool. When the cast is under way, a light pressure of the thumb on the bell of the reel keeps the cast under control. Or, as in the case of middle-spool thumbing, the thumb can be raised altogether.

From either position it is easy to stop the line at the end of the cast simply by pushing down hard against the line, or, as shown in picture No. 8, by pressing the side of the thumb firmly against the revolving bell or side of the reel. Notice in this picture how the line jumps back from the force of the quick stop, to drop the lure where aimed.

PICTURE NO. 6

PICTURE NO. 7

PICTURE NO. 8

THE CAST WITH STANDARD SURF REEL

The surf caster needs all the balance of a golfer and he uses some-what the same open stance. From the foot position shown in picture No. 9 he can pivot readily, all the while maintaining a good solid plant on the beach.

The unwary beginner may well catch more fishermen than fish. The first point he must learn is always to look back before he begins his cast, to be sure that his lure will not connect with some other angler or some natural object. In picture No. 10, Hal Lyman shows the approved position for the beginning of the cast, including that look over the shoulder.

Now he is ready, and the words to remember at this point are "pull" and "push." Close-up picture No. 11 shows how the reel handles are down, right thumb pressed lightly on the line to hold it tight, left hand gripping the rod butt. From this position the caster will PULL in with his left hand and PUSH outward with the right, in order to get the cast started with smoothness and power.

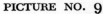

PICTURE NO. 9

177

PICTURE NO. 10

PICTURE NO. 11

In picture No. 12 the cast is just starting. The angler's feet are braced, the lure is in motion, the hands ready to push and pull. At the same time, the body starts to pivot from the hips. As the hip pivot comes around, in picture No. 13, the angler's arms are raised so the rod is coming up, preparatory to putting a snap into the cast.

As the angler's hips come away around in a perfect pivot, his right hand continues to push forward while his left hand pulls the butt of the rod in toward him. The arc of rod and moving plug shown in picture No. 14 is that formed just before the thumb is removed from the line on the spool, to send the plug on out. And in picture No. 15 the plug is sailing out over the ocean while the angler follows through with arm and body, meanwhile holding the thumb just off the reel, ready to clamp down and stop the cast if he should so wish.

The follow-through of the rod stops parallel to the beach, as shown in picture No. 16, so that the line can flow freely out through the top of the guides, thus avoiding friction.

PICTURE NO. 12

PICTURE NO. 14

180

THE RETRIEVE WITH STANDARD SURF REEL

When the lure hits the water, the angler quickly brings the butt of the rod down between his legs for steadiness, and the tip of the rod comes up, as shown in picture No. 17, both for better action on the retrieve and to absorb the shock of a possible strike. At the same moment he moves his left hand up, as in picture No. 18, to push the lever that puts the reel from free spool back into gear. The left hand

PICTURE NO. 17

then takes a grip forward of the reel, with left thumb hooked over the line to use as a level wind, as shown in picture No. 19.

In picture No. 20, Hal's right hand has moved to the reel handles and he is ready for the retrieve. He begins to reel, working the lure in, and if no strike occurs, as it nears the beach and he is almost ready to pick up for another cast, he points the rod well off to the right, as shown in picture No. 21. This is a safety angle, for if a fish should hit that close to the end of the retrieve, and if the retrieve is being made straight back to the angler, the lure might pull out of the fish's mouth and fly back at the fisherman at great speed and strike him in the face. And from the angle shown, it is easy to go into another cast.

PICTURE NO. 18

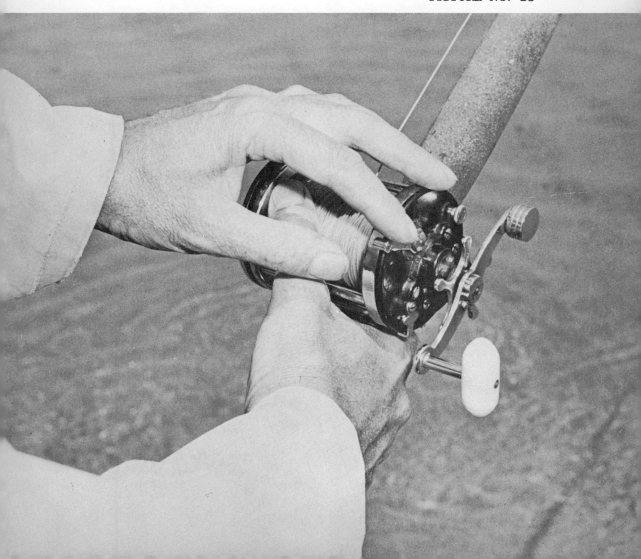

PICTURE NO. 19

PICTURE NO. 20

PICTURE NO. 21

SPIN CASTING IN THE SURF

The Grip   For casting in the surf with spinning gear, Frank Woolner advocates the grip shown in picture No. 22, two fingers of the right hand on each side of the shaft that holds the reel to the rod, while the left hand holds the cork well down toward the butt. The hands are spaced comfortably and the hold is not too tight, so that muscles may move smoothly and freely.

From this position, the forefinger of the right hand can readily pick up the line, as shown in picture No. 23. The weight of the lure

PICTURE NO. 22

or bait will then hold the line tight throughout the cast until such time as the caster allows it to slip off his finger and go on out. Once the lure is in the air, if he wishes to stop it, all he has to do is stick out his finger and pick the line up again, placing it on the knob, from which it can then be taken out by the run of a fish or reeled in by the angler.

Most surf casters who use spinning gear prefer this manual pickup type of reel rather than those which have a bail, because there is less manipulation of parts involved, and the line is not so likely to get fouled up.

PICTURE NO. 23

The Cast To begin the cast, surf fisherman Woolner pushes the rod rearward, in picture No. 24, right index finger holding the line, and the lure hanging down about 2½ feet below the rod tip. The rod is not pushed back as far as is the case with the open-faced surf reel shown in the previous series of photos, but goes only as far back as the angler can comfortably manage while keeping elbows down and wrists in position to give the required power to send the lure out a long distance.

As Frank begins the forward cast in picture No. 25, he brings the rod forward at about a 45-degree angle. The weight of the lure and the force of the start of the cast combine to put a good bend in the

PICTURE NO. 24

188

PICTURE NO. 25

rod, to furnish the whip needed to propel the lure forward at the proper time. Once again, as with the regular surf casting outfit shown on earlier pages, the left hand pulls in while the right hand pushes forward, in smooth combination, to make for effortless casting.

By the time he reaches the position shown in picture No. 26, the whole rod is working. At this very instant he releases the line from his finger tip and sends the lure shooting out over the water.

And in picture No. 27, as the lure reaches the spot where he wants it to land, he reaches out with his forefinger and catches the outgoing line. The lure is stopped and drops to the surface, and Frank puts the line back on the nub of the manual pickup, preparatory to re-trieving.

PICTURE NO. 27

The Retrieve with the Spinning Reel With the lure on the surface and the line on the nub of the reel, the caster shoves the butt of the rod between his legs to brace it, grasps the rod again with the same hand hold with which he started, two fingers on each side of the shaft, and begins the retrieve with the left hand, reeling forward to put line back on the spool, as shown in picture No. 28.

PICTURE NO. 28

The complete surf caster's gear—foul-weather jacket, waders, rods, sand spikes (holding rods), bill cap, spoons, plugs and plug holder, gaff and billy.